AWAKENING STARSEEDS

DREAMING INTO THE FUTURE, VOLUME 3

CURATED BY: RADHAA NILIA

Printed in the USA

To Our World - Planet Earth and her People!

CONTENTS

FOREWORD

"Here's to the crazy ones.
The misfits. The rebels.
The troublemakers.
The round pegs in the square holes.
The ones who see things differently.
They're not fond of rules.
And they have no respect for the status quo.
You can quote them, disagree with them,
glorify or vilify them.
About the only thing you can't do is ignore them.
Because they change things,
they push the human race forward.
And while some may see them as the crazy people
who are crazy enough to think
they can change the world,
are the ones who do."

-Steve Jobs.

A NOTE FROM THE TEAM:

We are a collective of artists, editors, formatters and dreamers who are inspired to share this Foreword for this third series of Awakening Starseeds. Some of us have chosen not to share our names, yet we have been working as a team throughout the series created by Radhaa Publishing House. We have always been inspired by the authors' courage to share their experiences and stories, regardless of how unconventional they are. We hope it inspires you to keep pushing through difficulties in your personal lives toward this challenging planetary shift from darkness to Light. It takes great fortitude to step forward and use your voice to claim what you know is your birthright. May this book remind you of who you are and activate the Seeds of Dharma (purpose) within you. We love you; that is why we curate these books. So thank you for your support as we ride the waves of ascension together. Keep Dreaming into a world you want. Blessings to you and all of Humanity for a Brighter Future!

Team Players at RPH

1

FUTURE ANCIENTS

BY: CAROLINE SECKINGER

"We are the Future Ancients"

We are the ones choosing the seeds to be cast out into the fields of chaos, the seeds that will code the Future. We are the ones to weave the threads of truth into the multidimensional fabric of the Future. We are the ones whose feet will dance the patterns that carve the Earth with our love. We are the ones clearing the rubble of the collapsing timelines of damaged personal, ancestral, and collective wounds. We are living in prophesied times, creating future myths. We are the ones to anchor the leylines of quantum consciousness into the alchemical compost of this collapse.

This collapse follows the order of the life cycles of these realms. Witches, shamans, mystics, visionaries, psychonauts, all those who are intimate with both the known and the unknown, the seen and the unseen, the Great Cycles drawn by the cosmos, the life cycle of a tree, recognize this collapse as inevitable.

There could be no other way here. The Divine Consciousness of this jewel planet, Gaia, has designed Her multidimensional realm of Earth to be so. Who knows what cycles constitute creation in other star systems or universes; but here in our corner of the mystery; She, Anima Mundi, Gaia as The Divine Feminine Manifest is directing the primal force in an unceasing cycle of creation, preservation, and destruction; pregnancy, birth, life, and death. Emerging and collapsing. Bloom and decay. Seed, sprout, fruit, rot, compost. There is no manifestation of Her sacred dream separate from these cycles. Here, the mountains collapse, the shorelines disappear, earthquakes and volcanoes swallow landscapes. So despite how powerful, seemingly solid, global, genius, glittering, engaging the pulsing world of human creativity and seduction appears, it too will grow, deconstruct and collapse.

Apocalypse: 'To Uncover, Reveal, Unveil'

This is the Great Turning. Gaia is evolving with us. She is expanding and contracting through this apocalypse to ascension, just as we are. How we choose to co-create in this apocalypse is how we will co-create with the next world. How we unveil the truth of our true co-creative power within creation is how we manifest the new world.

Humanity is so much younger than the mountains and the sea, the stars and the wind, the mysterious unnamable force that creates, permeates, and is all things. These ancient forces collaborate with us every moment of our being here. Our blood is the water, our breath the wind, our bones the minerals, our neurological firing, the fire. The elements are created by the cosmic design of great care. We are the co-creators of this reality, carrying the greatest power within us.

As I write this, I know that I don't know the entire truth. There is something liberating within the not knowing. Living in the mystery feels closer to living by the laws of magick. To create within this world of chaos is a form of alchemy.

Alchemy: *"The process of taking something ordinary and turning it into something extraordinary, sometimes in a way that cannot be explained."*

To live in truth, make beauty, love, and sustain life in a small corner of creation; is one of the greatest offerings we can make just now. If only to make an offering of love, within a breath. Love within the width of a breath is where I start and return every day. This is the ancient compost for the seeds.

How do we stay awake to the resonance of love within this chaos? The task to be in the collapse but not to collapse is no small one. To be so dislodged but to root and blossom in an environment that turns against life takes great discipline and intention. To cultivate and return to a state of love, curiosity, and growth while in a matrix designed to generate fear, illness, and confusion in as many ways as possible, is truly challenging, if not heroic. To harness the force of the seed released from a splitting pod that projects itself into the quantum field of possibility is a moment-to-moment alignment. We all carry ancestral wisdom of being deeply attuned to and aligned with the Earth as multidimensional beings. It is our birthright to be a vessel of divine awareness between heaven and Earth, form and formless, seen and unseen. Our task is to fill the crevices of the destruction, the decay with the frequency of our higher consciousness expressed as love, gratitude, generosity, and trust. This is how we become the co-creators with Gaia for generating the codes of the New Earth. To be a seed on Gaia is to contain the potential, magical, mystical, divine codes to grow into an expanded living form. We, too, contain the codes of seeds to be much grander, more expansive by aligning our cosmic intelligence with the primal force of creation in an earthly human seed body.

"A breath of love can take you to infinity."
— Rumi

There are moments when there may not be resources in our environment, psyche, families, or communities to draw upon, so this is when we seek to align with the forces behind what we are witnessing. We remember to not hold on to what is happening but to search for what is behind and before the events. We go back and go through until we touch upon something that radiates with a truth that provides clarity and peace. We turn our gaze inward to find the ancestral wisdom that has navigated oppression, destruction, and loss as we ask for this wisdom to guide us. We ask the benevolent wisdom beings in the other realms to ally with us. We cultivate a spiritual warrior's tool belt of skills and practices, including meditation, skillful prayer, self-care, boundaries, divination, gratitude, generosity, and receptivity. We remind ourselves, "There is more than what meets the eye," so we take the time to turn our gaze within to align with the quantum fields, witness the ancient patterns of creation, and anchor the incorruptible love from which we arose. These are some of the essential skills of a spiritual warrior.

Our attention and thoughts are our personal quantum tools for directing manifestation. How and where we place our attention is the generating force of our manifestation. When we attune to the consciousness of this planet, Gaia, and Her Original ancient forms, oceans, lakes, clouds, wind, soil, minerals, mountains, fire, plant life, i.e., we create leylines to the incorruptible power and original designs of this creation dream.

One of the greatest veils being lifted is to reveal our true nature as co-creators with what is incorruptible and divine within the physical and quantum realms. We can channel what is beyond the form of things, what is invisible, so that as form collapses, what we have manifested will remain.

Sovereignty: 'Freedom from External Control'

Claiming your spiritual and energetic sovereignty is one of the most powerful ways to travel through this apocalypse. The claiming of sovereignty is mastering your own veils, the down and dirty of knowing your wounds and shadows that have controlled or harnessed your perceptions of self, ancestral lines, collective consciousness, past lives, emotional, physical, and psychic bodies. It may include reckoning when these veils are the mechanisms by which you have found safety, survival, and made sense of a harsh, destructive inverted world. Some of our shadows are embedded in the infrastructure of our purpose, meaning, abundance, relationships, families, and communities. This is messy, difficult, disorienting, and lonely, yet necessary work. The lifting of your personal veils anchors you in your sovereignty. It is the ultimate shield of the spiritual warriors/warrioress.

Many awakenings occur when tragedy, illness, loss, or devastation occurs. We are in a collective tragedy and awakening. Those who are leading the way thru this rubble will invariably experience a major challenge to become carriers of the frequency of moving thru a collapse and arising like the phoenix awakened to one's power to grow, heal, co-create with the divinity of this universe, the primal force of creation, the quantum field is that which resides within all of us.

It is a great honor to be the initiators dawning the new world. Knowing this in our own unique way, to be in connection with the forces of creation, and the many manifestations and faces of the divine as multidimensional allies, is a powerful place to start. Quietly defying the forces that could close down, distract or misdirect our ability to connect with divinity and the infinite power of the quantum field is essential. We are to know ourselves as magnificent co-creators with the many faces of the divine, feminine and masculine in both form and formless. We are the conduits of truth that are shaping the new world.

My offering is to reawaken and deepen the relationship to the consciousness of Gaia, the primal force that exists within us, the unseen, and the quantum fields within the wisdom stored in our DNA. My work is to craft paths and leylines of the ancient deities of my European ancestors into the fabric of the now so that we may reconstitute the ancient true relationships to weave wisdom for the Future.

What I have to share about the other realms arises from my own practices. I honor your wisdom and perspective. My perception arises through my experience, and I know that is a very small thing. Every day what I believe I know changes actually. Bless your knowing. Your discernment is essential in the claiming of your spiritual sovereignty. You have traveled through many places, timelines, dimensions, worlds, and bodies to arrive in this place now, and I hope you will lean into your own sovereign wisdom.

Of the Deities I work with, some have extraordinary multidimensional gifts. Some, though divine, are also challenged with human traits like anger, jealousy, greed, betrayal, and lust. Some bless and benefit this realm of life, afterlife, and reincarnation with transcendent knowledge and gifts. Some have passed through trials that would endow them with supernatural traits. As I come to know these beings, I recognize that these myths, stories, and sacred narratives have traveled through our noosphere for millennia, encoded with ways to know ourselves and the other realm beings participating in this Earth theater. As we move into our sovereignty, we will recognize beings with different but not more access to the source of creation than we do. We are embodied in creation as form and divinity. We are of both worlds. I chose to work with the beings of other realms that do not hold dominion over us, and they respect our sovereignty by choosing to co-create with us. They are powerful. Indeed, they are older and wiser through time than we may be. Yet as we have incarnated into the smallest fraction of our true nature to act as fully divine beings, we need help, Especially now. Other realms, ancestors, magical beings, angels, gods and goddesses, star kin, and light beings are waiting to assist us. Even though these ties have been thwarted or twisted, inverted or cut off, they are ours to reclaim.

This knowledge has kept me in the practice of making these ceremonial tools. I work in bronze, silver, and gold, creating ceremonial tools that connect to the deities of my ancestors. I came into this metalwork a bit sideways. I had been using practices of women's labor (knitting, stitching, crocheting, sewing) to deepen my skills of prayer and mantra. After a few years between the fibers, tangible energy emerges. It was the beginning of imbuing the physical with an unseen field. While working, I heard the presence of my grandmothers through my DNA, their hands guiding mine as they too had once crafted blankets, sweaters, hats, and tunics 1000s of years ago. I sensed their approval and delight with my recognition of their labors that kept the baby warm, who too birthed a child, each life a tenacious stitch tying ultimately to mine. My reverence and gratitude grew for the dedication and perseverance to tending life each generation held. The conversations with my ancestors, within my hands, and the craft began to blur. The edges of matter, time, and energy were shifting. The conversations were so compelling that I began to practice ancestral healing. Soon I was aligned with four strong ancestors from my four ancestral lines; as sources of insight, love and guidance.

In 2018 I made my first ceremonial knife. A tool for spiritual warrioress. I was working with a leather knife and was drawn to the curved blade. It felt ancestral and feminine and fierce. I sought to forge leylines to my ancestral Pict, Celt, and Scandinavian indigenous spiritual fierceness. A few months later, I was commissioned to do a series of bronze sculptures. Bronze was a new medium for me, and my learning curve was steep. While attempting to form the wax into California native reptiles and being very frustrated, I asked for guidance on something that I could actually make in tears. The wax molded easily into a form, though I did not know it. I had to ask. All I heard was — a woman's ceremonial knife.

It was the first one, *"The Gaia Ceremonial Knife."* At first, I did not know how it was to be used or the significance, though it soon became clear. I now make a collection of ceremonial knives and pendants. Each is tied to a Deity or other realm of my ancestors embedded with the energetic codes of that other realm being. Each is related to an element of Earth, a dimension of Earth, or a galactic body. The Gaia Knife is in resonance with the consciousness of this precious planet, Gaia. As I work, metal is handled as a living bloodline of Gaia. I weave prayer, ceremony, ritual, and meditation practices into each piece. The Gaia Knife is to mend the wound of separation from divinity that is accessed through our connection to the frequency of the Earth.

Creating your own ceremonial relationship with the frequencies of Earth and Her cosmic alignment acknowledges that our physicality is innately part of a cosmic multidimensional celestial design.

Each of the beings I work with is a commission from the spirit world. These beings chose me before I chose them. I often don't know who they are. It takes time for me to sort through historical, mythological and, anthropological, meditative research before I understand who I will be working with. It can take months or even years before I will share a piece. I am often working outside of time. My prayer is that these knives be a note in the song of her mineral blood, to the muse of the ancients, as I am offering guidance on the path to remember our true selves in the co-creation with this glorious magical paradise planet Earth.

~

SAYING:

"The unconscious is also feared by those whose conscious attitude is at odds with their true nature. Naturally their dreams will then assume an unpleasant and threatening form, for if nature is violated she takes her revenge. In itself the unconscious is neutral, and its normal function is to compensate the conscious position. In it the opposites slumber side by side; they are wrenched apart only by the activity of the conscious mind, and the more one-sided and cramped the conscious standpoint is, the more painful or dangerous will be the unconscious reaction."

— C.G. Jung

CAROLINE SECKINGER

ABOUT THE AUTHOR

Caroline is an artist, mystic, psychonaut, activist, multidimensional guide, prayer conduit, ceremonialist, and solo witch. Her Life Is a Prayer. Her workbench is an Altar. The mountains, forests, rivers, and oceans are her Temples. The Stars are her Ancestors.

She crafts living ceremonial tools made through the ancient ways of lost wax casting in bronze, silver and gold. She imbues ceremony, prayer, and inter-dimensional leylines in her praxis; Her Eternal Ceremonial Knives.

She leads The Coherent Field Project, a meditation practice to harness the quantum intelligence of non-duality that arises through meditation into spiritual activism. She has guided thousands in ceremonial, prayer, and meditation practices.

Her artwork and films have been shown in galleries, collections, theaters, and film festivals worldwide, including public radio and PBS. Her work has been featured in SF Chronicle, California Home + Design, California Home, Design For Living, Sonoma Magazine, and several books, including Design By Nature (Erica Tanov) and California Modern (Gustave Carlson).

She has been the recipient of numerous awards, including: Andy Warhol Foundation for The Arts, Sony Corporation Visions Festival, Best Women's Film Cincinnati International Film Festival.

Her ceremonial tools are highly sought after in a growing tribe of knife-bearing priestesses.

www.carolineseckinger.com

2

REBEL WITH A CAUSE

BY: RADHAA NILIA

"The only way to deal with an unfree world is to become so absolutely free that your very existence is an act of rebellion."
— **Albert Camus**

I live in the Appalachian Mountains. I never imagined living on the *'Trail of tears* or even in North Carolina. I was obsessed with living in the middle of the City of Angels, AKA LA. I had a serious case of FOMO (Fear Of Missing Out). I was in the mix of it all when a rumbling came into my life. Spirit guided me out of the City, telling me to give away all my belongings and move onto the top of Crystal Mountain. It was hard to process these very direct instructions. When I moved to LA in my 20's, starting as a model while taking the Producer's program, I had big dreams and was working my way up. I struggled every step of the way. It was hard and laborious work, but I never complained because I believed that making movies was the epitome of Success. The ability to reach people worldwide and tell stories through films motivated me. So I moved to the City of Dreams to become a filmmaker.

City of Dreams — Hollywood

Hollywood is the land of creativity. Every creative person with ambition flocks to this City of Dreams. It's the honeypot of seduction for creatives. I couldn't help but be seduced. The lure of Success hypnotized me. And boy, I wanted it so badly, I was willing to work overtime.

I met so many influential people in my life in Hollywood, to the point that I found myself sitting across the table from Harvey Weinstein. It was at a film event. I did some PR work and sat at a table talking to actors. They were all so excited because Harvey Weinstein was there. I looked at him, and he looked at me, we locked eyes, and he walked straight over to me. Harvey Weinstein didn't want to sit and talk to the other actors, who were all drooling to have their chance to meet him. He wanted to speak to me away from the group and invited me to his table. He was very charming and inquisitive, wanting to know why I was there. I explained I was doing some PR work, but my real goal was to be a Producer. He nodded, and he could tell I had what it took.

He wanted to meet with me about the possibility of working for his company and told me he would send his assistant to get my information. The assistant was nowhere to be found, I didn't see her anywhere in sight, but to my surprise, she seemed to appear out of nowhere after our lengthy conversation. A bright and bubbly blond who knew how to get down to business arrived. I could feel success at my fingertips.

Companies I worked with loved hiring me because I knew how to negotiate and get the best deals on locations, catering, equipment, tools, and everything we needed to make a film as a Producer.

This was before all the news breaking on Harvey and the #metoo movement. It was, in fact, right before this all broke loose. Because at that moment, Harvey still carried the untouchable crown, *"God of Hollywood,"* per Meryl Streep.

Rebelling Against the Game

Everything was within reach if I was willing to play the game. The only problem was that I found myself rebelling from the game. I found myself running away from it, even though it was what I thought I wanted with every fiber of my being. And yet, something was breaking open inside of me, asking myself whether I was ready to go all in. I was told many times that there was only one way up. It was almost a scolding that higher-ups said. We were all supposed to be grateful to breathe the same air as those who had *'made it,'* but I didn't feel that way. As I got to know the affluent and famous as friends and associates, I was already seeing behind the veil. Many were not happy at all. There were problematic themes such as severe insomnia, that they had to be on heavy sleeping pills, and had equally severe addictions: Sex, drugs, shopping, plastic surgery, you name it.

I admit that a part of me was also numbing in this toxic environment of illusion. I felt I had to cut off my naturally intense emotions. And strange things were happening that shook me to my core. I experienced traumatic experiences that confused me. But despite the insanity of Hollywood culture, I was still able to maintain my Soul. A force larger than me intervened in my life. A Kundalini Awakening was taking place amidst all this. It felt like I was in the eye of the storm, being swept by both sides of reality. My internal and external reality was not matching. Because the truth was, I valued my freedom above all. And the fear of being trapped in a realm I wasn't ready to commit terrified me.

My Hollywood Experience

I was offered an opportunity that some would die for, which I passed up at the time because the proposition was hard on my Soul. For many, this would be a dream come true. I was getting enticing offers that would change my life forever and potentially place me at the top of my game as a Producer had I played my cards right.

So what would playing my cards '*right*' mean in clear English? A set of rules was required, and they were simply '*known*' to those who were part of the game. We, the workers, were to turn a blind eye to every abuse that occurred in the workplace. It would mean keeping all the secrets of the casting couch, of how Executives brought in talent without hiring them, but making them come in and do special favors for promises of a better future. It meant saying nothing as they harvested money from endless investors who were only partially assigned to the projects but mostly to themselves. It meant being mute and blind but only speaking when doing something that would move the company or project forward. It would also mean being available at any day or hour for any reason to serve the higher-ups. And to be a good fit for this job, I would have to shut down all my senses and empathy and become a cold-hearted human, like a robot.

I was working with several studios when something woke me up from inside me in the face of all my dreams. A stirring that was unstoppable. I had a spiritual awakening that brought the Dark Night to my Soul. I asked myself, *"What am I doing? Who am I doing this for? What is my real purpose?"* I was helping to make other people's dreams come true with films I didn't even believe in. The films and projects I was working on were far from what I had originally dreamed. I felt like I was drowning in a nightmare of illusions. There was something that didn't feel right in my Soul. It stopped me from pursuing a dream career that I had thought of for a very, very long time to be the most important asset of my life — a Producer in Hollywood. Only to have all my Producer's credits not included or all together deleted on IMDB and the films. Deleted from films that were coming out I had worked tirelessly on and were in post-production. I was deleted, thrown in the trash, and discarded. As if I never existed. Just like that.

Here's how it all happened. In one of the studios, I worked under the supervision of an executive who had taken an obsessive liking to me. He invited me on vacation and insisted I should go. I declined. I did not think much of it since I was burnt out and worn from working so hard. I was not interested in anyone, nor did I have the energy to date. He kept telling me, *"I could rise to the top if I were more cooperative."* He asked me to spend extra time with him, but I had no extracurricular activities and extra time to spend as I was working overtime. Even more aggressive as the high executive, his partner was tormenting and womanizing every woman who worked there. We have already worked so hard, and on top of it, trying to dodge unwanted advances and abuse daily.

My unwillingness to cooperate in ways they demanded and required did not please them. And the same Hollywood executive called me to tell me, *"You're officially blacklisted in Hollywood! You will never work again in the industry!"*

He also announced that, *"He knew everything and everyone!"*

In short, I was blocked and could not ever enter Hollywood again.

I had completed five films where I gave my blood, sweat, and tears — my life force. And now, it was as if I had never existed. For one year, I couldn't move and talk. I got very ill. The trauma of being suppressed, silenced, and deleted from all the creative projects I have worked so hard for was devastating. No one stood up for me. I felt alone and isolated, and there was no one I could talk to with all the pain and suffering I had experienced. To have created all these films that suddenly turned dust in the winds. I felt deserted in a desert of deprivation. The betrayal felt like a thousand swords in my back. To think that I have worked with so many people, people I thought were my friends, in the end, I had no real allies. They were all too busy trying to move up the ladder themselves.

Gang Stalking

Even after all of this, letting go of my Hollywood connections, I had been targeted. I was getting gang stalked. A person or a group would follow me for hours--wherever I went and whatever I did. If I went to a restaurant, they sat in front of me and stared without blinking with the intention of intimidation to cause distress: a tactic used by the Dark that is far more common than people think. Most people don't know this type of harassment exists, yet it is a common tool for the Hollywood Cabal. I had some pretty serious events that occurred after as well. Someone *'randomly'* ran into my brand new, fully paid-off car while it was parked in the middle of the night in West Hollywood. They totaled it in one clean swipe. I called the police, but they never actually came. The man who had hit my car was picked up by someone else and swept away within minutes of the crash. My place was ransacked, and the diamond ring I bought for myself to represent self-love and all my sentimental value things and jewels was taken. I had four computers stolen, one after another, along with my purse and phone. It was a nightmare! When I turned my back on the monsters, they came after me. And they let me know with so many ways that I was not safe and that my life would be hell because I would not submit. I would never submit to these pathetic tactics. But they wanted me and my loyalty. Even though I was cast out, they expected me to turn around, get down on my knees, and beg. To beg and beg and beg until they felt I had submitted so thoroughly that I would learn my lesson. But all they would hear is NO, again and again.

It was all a game in the first place, and it was to make me so sorry that I would do ANYTHING for a small insignificant place in that hell hole. This did not interest me in the least bit. The attacks came in a variety of ways. But one of the most consistent ways was through *"Black Magic."* The occult runs deep here.

The losses were great. Even when I started these book series, there was a lot of interference. Once we had completed and finished everything from editing to formatting, there was always scrambling at the end of the work. Chapters would change, and words would be missing, taken out, or misspelled. Everything in the book was distorted the first time we completed Awakening Starseeds, Vol. 1. We had to upload the book ten times. And ten times, we had to edit and reformat it. My team was in tears. They wanted to give up. I couldn't understand how we could upload a clean version and turn it into a dirty one. For a moment, I felt the 'Dark' blocked me. As if to tell me, *"Don't you dare be successful on your own. Don't you dare. All attempts will be sabotaged."*

This continued for two years of my startup at my Publishing House. We would all look at the clean version of our book and upload it together as a team. As if solidified, all eyes had seen the clean version. Then when we ordered the printed version in paperback, it would be scrambled again.

We were hit with other horrific anomalies, one being that our key team player's dog and my dog got very sick at the same time -- both our dogs died a week apart. My dog had black goo on various parts of her body. I went to over half a dozen vets, and no one could identify what was going on with her. Bella, my furry companion, was the love of my life. Losing her put me in a state of inconsolable grief. My book teammate also had a severe car accident in LA and had to retire from working on these books. These are the tactics that the dark use to break down our spirit and mission.

And although, the grief was overwhelming, nothing could sway me from the truth. I knew that even if my heart was bleeding, that my mission was just getting started. And because of my devotion to the Divine, no matter what came my way, whatever was stolen from me, or how much these soulless beings physically harassed me and tried to torment me or messed with my projects, I knew the Divine protected me. There was an armor of God that shielded me. It made me fearless in the face of such horrific events. These attacks only put me on the path of my own mastery. My faith grew and learning so many healing modalities and techniques over the years only strengthened me. Later, I learned how weak demons truly are.

You see, they can only feed off the *'fears'* of people. They cannot create anything original. Instead, they use highly creative people to harvest energy and ideas and always claim them as their own. The Dark has enslaved too many creatives and brilliant souls. If you see people going crazy in Hollywood, now you know why. A strong mind and determined Soul must rise above these mind control techniques. But most importantly, it takes giving yourself fully over to the true Creator, because ONLY in that space are you truly protected.

Walking the Path of a Tantrika

A Tantrika is willing to let go of everything. Every identity and belief that prevents one from living according to the Divine will. Hollywood had blocked me, now I was willing to delete all the false identities I had taken on. I was willing to become a blank canvas and allow the mystery of life to paint my brand-new reality.

I had to surrender to trust the higher power pulling me forward. It was an initiation into becoming a *'Tantrika.'* I knew my calling and service were larger than being an enslaved person. I knew that my life-force energy that brought many projects together is my manifesting power and that I can now harness it for projects I believe approved by the Divine. It doesn't matter if my projects become with the masses or not," because it's meant for those who will resonate and understand the deeper messages I produce.

'Tantra' is a fight between the dark forces and light warriors. "Tantrik or Tantrika" are warriors of Light, merging with the Divine (not necessarily with others). A Tantrika is in greater service to a spiritual mission than oneself. Being a Tantrika is not about finding pleasure in rotating sexual partners (a distorted belief Westeners latched on). It is not about sexual thrills at all. It is far deeper. It is about having union with the

Creator. Tantra is about emptying a cup filled by mind control programming and filling it up with the Divine.

What I had experienced was indeed a tantric experience. I walked through darkness to understand both light and dark better. But when I had learned what I needed to learn, the Dark pushed me out of its hell realm, casting me out as our energies were no longer a match. And out of the deepest love of the Creator, I was taken far away and put into a magical spot on the top of the mountains where Light and love are flourishing within me and my environment.

What a powerful tantric initiation. One where I found myself face to face with darkness. I danced with the devil, but I never sold my Soul. I walked away, and yes, part of me died. I was being pulled to go deeper into the feminine mysteries within myself. I had an inner calling to start writing. And then, I was called to curate books for Starseeds. After my this experience, I knew I would never be mainstream, that I was choosing the life of an Indie. I was choosing freedom. I knew I would not have the backing of the studios, companies, or corporations. I became a rebel with a cause. I was determined to thrive with my own creations and work with the Creator instead. I was moving forward with a purpose. And so, my rebirthing began.

Released from Darkness

I share this very personal story with you because I have witnessed many people stuck in darkness, believing it was the only way to get what they wanted. Only to regret it later but never have the courage to live on their terms. I am here to tell you that it is not only possible, but it's your birthright to be Sovereign and free.

Even when you experience the dark night of your Soul, you can and will come through it. There is a part of you, so radiant, so alive, that has been covered with the programming we have all received by being born on this planet of the 3rd dimension, but things are rapidly changing now.

Unexpected Blessings

After moving to the Appalachians, I was being creative on my own, and I thought, why not submit a film I had Directed and Produced as a female filmmaker? I remember getting a call that I was up for the 'Alice Guy Blanche Award,' nominated as one of the best female Directors in New Jersey. I was invited to the screenings and the award show. It meant so much to me to be included in the top tier of female Directors, and even though I didn't walk with the award, I felt like a winner. Soon after, I won Best Director at Indie Fest in Los Angeles, which I didn't attend because I was on the East Coast working on other projects. But I was grateful and surprised to discover I had won. I realized I didn't have to be in the mix of it all, especially in the City of LA. I didn't need to be accessible to everyone. As I realized my job was to create and be creative, the work would be found. I let go of all the ways I was told things must be done, allowing the Creator to carry through me new doors full of even bigger blessings.

"Awaken to who You are,
Reclaim your inner knowing
Your own inner power.
Reclaim every part of your Soul,
Call back all your Soul fragments,

Call on the Divine to help you
Release yourself from the bondages of this reality.
We are riding the waves to higher realms,
Though, at times, it may look bleak outside.
It is time to look within.
You can be free
Through your very own God's spark light.
Please don't give up for a moment.
I invite you to Dream into the Future.
You have a choice to align with the Divine.
It's never too late to find your way back.
Trust, you will be supported every step of the way."
—Radhaa

Creating My Publishing House

After my Soul searching and the healing journey I went through in releasing deep deprogramming and many of the false beliefs and illusions I had taken on, I realized how mind-controlled I had been. I realized I could make an impact without compromising my core values. I am thankful to understand my values so much better after these intense experiences. I was horrified after the fact but grateful that the Creator guided me back home and provided the miracles for my healing and realization of what I truly wanted, *"To be close to the Creator, be of service through my creativity."*

I didn't want to play anyone's games anymore. I didn't participate in things that didn't feel right. I had so much anger and pain from dealing with monsters in the industry that I didn't realize how much I needed to get away until I had left it all behind.

Hollywood is the land of glamorous slavery, and I didn't want to be enslaved. I didn't want to be abused, dishonored, and left with nothing but a shell of myself. I wanted to do the opposite. I wanted to collect all the gems of my Soul back and clear myself from the mind virus rampant, and all consume those involved. I wanted to use my life force for something beautiful. I wanted to serve the sacred. I wanted to share my voice and help others authentically share their voices. I didn't want to hide my precious Soul. I was tired of pretending to be somebody I wasn't. I was tired of a pretentious lifestyle and didn't want to keep up with anybody or live up to anyone else's standards. I wanted to honor my Sovereign Truth.

Manifesting in the Mountains

The spirit of the mountains changed me or perhaps let me simply be more of who I truly am. The quartz crystals underneath the land activated me. My mom and I reprogrammed them together to create peace and harmony. We worked with the spirits of the land, and it started to give me back so much more of what I needed. Through Shamanic rituals and incantations, I received back my Soul fragments and created manifestations of new realities. It's my secret to manifesting power. My choices in working with the lay lines, land grids, and elemental forces, are so powerful beyond our comprehension that I could have a one-pointed focus. The *"Awakening Starseeds"* book series is a part of my creation. I established Radhaa Publishing House, which was created in a way that felt good to me, while I was teaching at Goddess Code Academy™ with my healing modality, Goddess Activations™. It brought me so much fulfillment and purpose to share these creations with others from my heart. And nothing can compare to doing what you love when it's aligned with your Soul.

Embracing Sustainability

Something shifted in me living in the Appalachians. I started to think more about sustainability. In part, becoming more sovereign meant learning simpler ways to start living off the grid. I felt like I was a pioneer in these wild and untouched mountains. The wildness helped to bring back my wild woman.

"There is a wild that lives in all of us, NOT the rockstar wild, but the ancient primordial wild in its full aliveness."

The trees helped shield the collective consciousness, and my mind settled down. It wasn't constantly interrupted by the broadcast messages that pulsed into this World.

I was clueless about living more sustainably, yet I knew I was open to learning more. The word Sustainable has been a trendy topic for this decade. But what does that phrase mean? When I lived in LA, I thought sustainability meant getting a Prius. I got two of them, brand new. But unfortunately, they both got hit and totaled within six months of purchase, so I thought it was a sign to go in a different direction, and I ended up getting an SUV, which I loved and had for years. It was solid, reliable, and great for mountain living. I stopped needing the latest trends and moved out of the matrix of having to keep up with the Joneses.

I was so far from being cool, and it was a relief. I thought less about things and appearance. I even grew dreadlocks for not combing my hair while deeply writing my book and not trying to impress anyone. Simply being! Walking through the forest brought me immense peace in my heart and mind. I knew that I wanted to get to know nature in the way I had loved as a child in the Cordillera mountains of the Philippines when I had lived in such harmony with Mother Earth. My Soul was being called to come back to nature and to remember my roots, I was always the daughter of the mountain.

Sustainability is the practical conscious approach to minimizing the use of Earth's resources and its impact on our environment's consumption of things and less footprint by conserving to support long-term generational planetary resources for our Future. The few sustainable, practical ideas I've been thinking of: creating a Vegetable garden, planting seeds for a better future, and Bartering. Having natural resources and living a simple life in a time where the saying goes, *"Simple Living High Thinking,"* feels right.

My Vision for the Future

There is no doubt that the timelines have split. I see that people have more desire to get in touch with Mother Earth. Moving out of the smart cities, instead choosing to create smaller communities and sustainable living, having more time to be plugged into the Divine in all they do. As a natural storyteller and trained Filmmaker, I see myself bringing stories that activate emotional and spiritual intelligence, feeding humanity's thirst for exploring their own deeper existence. I envision the creatives, the rebels, and the Starseeds awakening into their specific missions and leadership roles. I envision new tools for healing that are organically advanced, such as med beds and so many more innovations for our Future. People will be led to the experiences they need to experience to evolve further. It's time for us to start Dreaming about our Future and where we are going with all of this.

Today, Radhaa Publishing House is a very important medium to convey stories of truth. We've already reached thousands of people across the lands, and it's only growing. I see that the Future is Brighter than we could ever imagine, and I look forward to all that is to come. My job has been a transmitter, an energy alchemist, and in helping remind others that they are alchemists too.

I envision more people willing to go deeper to explore individual healing. Because if we want to live in a more peaceful, inclusive, sustainable, and just World, it begins with each of us. As long as we continue to walk the path of denial, we'll be unable to heal ourselves, unable to resolve the past or fully live into our purpose for being here. Because let's face it, we're living in crazy times. There's no doubt about it. Of course, there is evidence to the contrary, yet it feels like it's becoming increasingly challenging to be optimistic. Yet we're being triggered to our core by what we see, hear, feel, and sense. It's clear to see there is a collective of excessive and unprocessed anger, inconsolable grief, isolation, sadness, and fear within us individually and collectively. Yet, we have the power to counter that by doing our own inner work. As we go deep within we crack the healing codes and bring a Universal healing back into our World.

Times are changing. And yet I know that the Light has already won. The Drama is just playing out. Everything will shift, including the Entertainment industry, and when it comes back, it will benefit all of humanity's consciousness. If you see the World tumbling down around you, don't tremble but stand tall, for all will pass. We are learning to return to our true nature as we plant the Seeds of Change.

Much love, *~Radhaa*

RADHAA NILIA

ABOUT THE AUTHOR

Radhaa Nilia is a Feminine Leader, Author, and the Creatrix of 'Goddess Code Academy.'

Radhaa's mission and vision are to serve women through holistic education and empowerment through Goddess Code Academy™. A mystical school for the Divine Feminine where she teaches her signature modality Goddess Activations™. .

'Goddess Code Academy' is A Mystical school for the Divine Feminine. It is an online temple where she teaches her original modality, Goddess Activations™. A healing method to Awaken and Activate Goddess Codes™, which helps clear negative beliefs, blockages, and lineage wounds while awakening the long-dormant codes. With a passion for Healing and Story-telling, Radhaa's otherworldly guidance had her create Radhaa Publishing House. A heart-centered Publishing company that focuses on collaborative books for up-and-coming authors. Email Radhaa.nilia@gmail.com.

To find Radhaa go to: www.RadhaaNilia.net

3

MAHARLIKA: IN SEARCH OF IDENTITY

BY: DEO PALMA

"Humanity is ONE and Indivisible."
— **P.R Sarkar**

I was born in Maharlika (known as the Philippines). I became a social service worker and provider to the less fortunate during my travels to many places worldwide where my service is needed. I first met Shrii P.R. Sarkar in Lake Gardens, West Bengal, India, in 1986, where we had a deep conversation. He told me, *"Humanity is bleeding, and I should do concrete things for humanity."* I learned about PROUT's spiritual and social philosophy (Progressive Utilization Theory). Three years later, in 1989, I met Sarkar again in Tiljala, Calcutta, and he instructed me, "*Go and do your duty!*" It was an extraordinary experience having a one-on-one meeting with this great personality. I embraced P.R. Sarkar's teachings in this context.

WHAT is PROUT?

PROGRESSIVE UTILIZATION THEORY (PROUT) was propounded by P.R. Sarkar in 1959, a new socio-economic-political philosophy. PROUT philosophy is a fusion between non-carbonic and carbonic Fabula, completeness, and universal outlook. This philosophy gives a completely new direction for social reconstruction. It considers humans as spiritual beings and explains all the laws of social movement. While framing social laws and systems, care has been taken to safeguard human values. In this relative world, everything is altering. "Any social system must give a method to new ideas if it fails to safeguard human values. Progress denotes well-adjusted growth of life's physical, mental, and spiritual aspects." This progressive idea is the essence of Prout's philosophy. Prout's philosophy is fundamentally opposed to Capitalist and Marxist ideas. It is also fundamentally opposed to human society's religious, nationalist, and racialist divisions.

On one of Sarkar's visits to the Philippines on August 21, 1971, he informed the Filipinos through one of the contemporary thinkers from the Philippines named Carbonel, *"That the pre-colonial name of the Philippines was Mahárliká."* This was a revealing moment for Carbonel. (At that moment, there was an incident of hand grenades being thrown in Plaza Miranda that caused 15 deaths; eight of them were children. Among those wounded was Former senator Eddie Ilarde, the founding chairman of the Mahárliká Movement). While Sarkar was explaining to him the true meaning of Mahárliká, the contemporary thinker said that there would be an impending revolution in the country.

Maharlika, Dreaming Sovereign & Free

Maharlika has been under the multiple waves of shifts from one form of conquest to another, creating an imbalance in all aspects of life where people were misinformed and under-educated about their true identity. Gaining a proper perspective of their origin allows them to remember their relationship with *'Inang Bayan'* - Mother Land. The country name *'Maharlika'* gives strength to the people. 'Philippines,' was a corrupt name given to the country by conquerors and therefore does not resonate with people's true identity. In my upcoming book, *"Maharlika - In Search of Identity 2,"* it is crucial to learn more about human nature and the various bloodlines running through the veins of the people of mixed races like ours to understand where we have been and where we are going as people. My understanding of PROUT philosophy allows me to share this precious knowledge to awaken my people and humanity in this quickening of the transformation taking place on Earth at this time.

Key Policies of PROUT:

1. Guarantee of Minimum Necessities of Life

According to the philosophy of PROUT, all persons should be guaranteed the minimum necessities of life, such as food, clothing, education, housing, and medical care. This is the most fundamental right of all people. What is the use of a man's right to vote if this does not lead to the right to live and feed his/her family?

In the capitalist system, this is countered by the argument that *"Everybody has an equal opportunity to become rich."* This is patently false, as a poor, uneducated farmer living in a poor rural community has practically no chance of making it, while a well-educated son of a rich man living in a metropolis has a very good chance to become rich.

The right to the fundamental necessities of life should be guaranteed in the country's constitution, not as charity but as an opportunity to be earned through one's work. a.) If someone chooses not to work, it does not mean his/her necessities should not be guaranteed. b.) Anyone willing to put in a full day's honest work should be entitled to a better wage. c.) Of course, disabled, sick, and elderly people may be exempted from the requirement to work if their condition warrants it. Without compromising democratic freedoms, this might sound like a 'Utopia.' If we look at the history of the world, a simple calculation shows that it is quite feasible. The main problem is that of distribution. The world is rich enough, and we produce enough goods to take care of the basic necessities of life for everybody. Some people simply consume too much of the world's resources.

In terms of per capita income, for example, Cuba is economically poorer than Mahárliká, yet judged by all other social indicators, it is better off. Child mortality is lower; the number of doctors per capita is higher; poverty is lower; educational standards are higher. So what is the difference? Income distribution is fairer, and society invests in people's basic needs.

We naturally do not want a communist dictatorship like what Cuba has, where cell phones were banned, and basic liberties curtailed. Yet, Cuba undoubtedly demonstrates that even in a poor country, it is possible to allocate resources in such a way that nobody needs to go hungry, and everybody has the minimum requirements of life.

The Scandinavian countries are also good examples of democratic rich countries where everyone's minimum needs are taken care of. That was what I understood decades ago during my visit, but with conditions changing fast in our world, time, place, and leaders can change such realities after the pandemic was installed.

2. Limitation to the Accumulation of Wealth

As the guaranteeing of minimum necessities for all is tightly connected with the distribution of wealth, it is clear that it is incompatible with the unlimited accumulation of wealth by a few individuals. You cannot guarantee everyone's minimum necessities if you allow the unlimited wealth accumulation in a few individuals' hands. For argument's sake, if one person were to accumulate all the planet's wealth, it would be impossible for anyone else to get enough to survive. Therefore, guaranteeing minimum necessities with a restriction on the accumulation of wealth goes hand in hand.

This does not mean that everyone will get the same. This cannot happen in reality. There will always be those that are better off than others due to chance, hard work, special talents, and other superior human qualities. What has to be prevented is that a small group of rich people accumulate so much wealth that others have to starve.

*"In a '**Proutist society**', everybody will be guaranteed the minimum necessities, but not more. From there on, everybody is provided the proper environment if they wish to acquire more wealth and improve their standard of living. However, if any person is about to acquire so much wealth that it will prevent others from getting their minimum requirements, society will have to step in and prevent such hoarding."*

—

3. Utilization of Resources

A healthy society is a constantly increasing standard of living for everyone, with the gap between the richest and poorest becoming narrower. Two things are required to achieve this for the population as a whole. First, we need to utilize the resources of this planet in increasingly efficient ways, and secondly, we need to distribute those resources rationally.

Mahárliká has enormous natural wealth in land, coastlines, minerals, forests, rivers, plains, and the like. In the past, most of these have been exploited shortsightedly, with much of the rainforests being destroyed and natural resources depleting. Maximum utilization of a thing does not mean raping it and destroying it but nurturing it so it will produce wealth for generations to come. It means sustainable utilization of our natural resources. If shortsighted profit is the motive, we will end up destroying the earth that feeds us. We can utilize and allocate resources much better if we take a longer vision.

By the term *'resources,'* we do not mean solely physical resources but mental and spiritual resources. For example, a lack of education reduces people's ability to utilize their mental faculties. While intelligence might be inborn, knowledge is definitely not. Without knowledge, even the most intelligent person cannot achieve much.

Therefore, an educated population has an enormous advantage in improving the living standard of all. An educated population leads to greater technological innovation, which improves the production of food and other products.

4. Preventing the Drainage of Wealth

In this world, riches tend to flow from poor areas to rich

areas. This is true between countries, such as the flow of valuable natural resources from third world countries to the industrialized ones, as well as within countries. In this case, valuable resources usually flow from rural areas to rich towns and cities. One way to do this is through the current terms of trade. The prices of agricultural produce are kept low, while those of industrialized goods are pushed high. This is not a natural phenomenon but the direct result of a manipulation of the markets.

Today, large corporations use huge fishing fleets to deplete the fish along the coastlines of Mahárliká, so local fishermen can hardly survive. This is another type of drainage of resources.

Commenting on poverty in the rural areas of the Mahárliká, Arsenio M. Balisacan states:

"The large income disparity between Luzon and the rest of the country, as well as between urban and rural areas, has attracted much attention in policy discussions. The common theme emerging from these discussions is that the disparity is largely responsible for the high income inequality in the country, implying that much of the inequality would be reduced by policy reforms aimed at closing the income gap between regions and between rural and urban areas."

The drainage of wealth from one area to another is the main reason poverty is widespread worldwide. The idea of 'economic assistance' and 'help to the third world is a bit of a misnomer because, despite the assistance offered by the rich countries to the poor, there is a bigger and more constant flow of resources from poor countries to the rich ones.

"Under PROUT, all such drainage of wealth would be stopped. Profits and wealth generated in one area would be plowed back into that

area, thus increasing living standards in poor countries and rural areas.”

5. Cooperatives

It is clear from capitalism that allowing private firms and big corporations to rule the economy leads to extreme concentrations of wealth in the hands of the few and poverty for the many. On the other hand, if a central government tries to run all factories and businesses, we will end up with a centralized and inefficient bureaucracy like that of the former Soviet Union. So what is the alternative? The simple answer is cooperatives!

A cooperative is a private business owned by its workers. This provides the best of all worlds in that it provides the incentives of a capitalist system without the extreme concentrations of wealth. Also, it would be the ultimate resolution to the Marxist conflict between workers and capitalists, as the cooperative merges the two into one!

Some operations might be too small or too impractical to run as cooperatives. A one-man barber shop would not make sense as a cooperative, as it would be a cooperative of one person! Therefore under PROUT, small farms, small family businesses, and businesses that employ very few individuals could still be owned by private individuals without negatively affecting the economy. Gradually, small farms must join with other farms to make efficient cooperatives.

Finally, large, capital-intensive industries would be better left in the hands of state benevolent governments. Their objective should be primarily to provide public services and not to make a profit. Power-generating companies, public utilities, banks, mining, and establishments producing raw materials would be prime examples of such companies.

6. Leadership

Defective leadership is one of the main causes of misery in human society. People blindly follow even the unintelligent leaders who hypnotize and attract thousands with their tall talks, gestures, and other dramatics. You should know that the poverty and misery of people in any country are caused by the sins or failures of their leaders. True leaders should always be vigilant and think about how to work best for human society; they must be cautious that under their guidance, the people are not led to darkness, death, and immorality. (Supreme Expression, II, 143)

The viability of democracy rests on an electorate possessing three factors: (1) education, (2) socio-economic and political consciousness, and (3) moral integrity. For a benevolent government, leaders need to be morally principled and dedicated to serving society. Authority should not be concentrated in the hands of individuals but should be expressed collectively.

7. Freedom

Individuals should have complete freedom to acquire and express their ideas, creative potential, and inner aspirations. Such intellectual and spiritual freedom will strengthen the collective interest. Ideally, human freedom should be greater than it is in most current societies, with the condition that one's actions must not harm others. Restrictions should only be placed on actions clearly detrimental to the welfare of others. If one's actions hurt oneself and others, then such a person requires proper counseling and education and inspiration and guidance from alternative character-building activities.

8. Cultural Diversity

PROUT encourages protecting and cultivating local culture, language, history, and tradition in the spirit of universal fellowship. For social justice and a healthy social order, cultural diversity is encouraged because diversity is an inherent quality of the human race. Alongside the development of local culture, Proutists also seek to create and encourage a universal culture that gathers all positive elements of all cultures. It also supports a universal language every person can learn, while encouraging all local languages and dialects.

9. Women's Rights

PROUT's goal is coordinated cooperation and equal rights between men and women. PROUT encourages the struggle against all forms of violence and exploitation against women. Furthermore, PROUT seeks the economic, social, and spiritual empowerment of women worldwide. Women especially need to take on greater leadership responsibility in every sector of society.

PROUT stands to create a powerful, dynamic, and elevating social consciousness, especially among women, so that they are inspired to rise, abolish dogma, annihilate all forms and symbols of slavery, and usher in a new era of coordinated cooperation and glorious achievement. "Women should be the vanguard of the new revolution humanity must undertake to achieve a glorious tomorrow."

10. Science and Technology

Scientific knowledge and technology are potential assets of

humanity if used properly; technology reduces physical hardship, thus providing people with more time for cultural pursuits and self-development. However, the development and utilization of scientific knowledge must come under the guidance of humanistic and spiritual values and moral leadership. Otherwise, technology may be abused by profiteers and power-hungry, resulting in destruction and exploitation. Such examples are the weapons of mass destruction developed using high technology, all done in the name of national security and protecting a rich country's interests.

Practical Policies "We, as the People" would like to Implement in Maharlika Now

---

Even though fundamental changes cannot be done without a Proutist economic system in place, much can and should be done right now to alleviate the difficulties of the common Mahárliká/s. Here are some specific demands that should be put forward to the governance policy framework:

1. Expand the domestic market by giving people more purchasing power. Increase the minimum wage. For any company that decides it cannot or will not pay the new minimum wage, provide an option for the workers to take over the ownership of the company as a cooperative. Tighten the laws against contract workers, so large corporations like large shopping malls are bound to give their workers the benefits they are entitled to by law. Invest heavily in education, skills training, and human resources. Carry out the land reform that was started during the Aquino administration in the way it was initially intended, and remove the loopholes that allowed landowners to escape from their responsibilities. Promote coop-

eratives and give incentives to people that wish to form cooperatives.

2. Dismantle elite democracy and monopoly of family dynasties. As they are using corporations that are mostly financed by bank loans and should be taken away from the control rule of the elite who are not using their own money, but money created by the banks, it is immoral that they should derive the benefits from resources that do not belong to them. Redistribute all vast land holdings. Steps must be taken so that all types of lobbying by rich corporations shall be banned and that the political system is removed from the influence of the wealthy

3. Stop environmental degradation and the exploitation of the mining, timber, and fishing industries. Specific actions can be designed to promote this goal by targeting companies polluting the environment and exploiting local residents.

Lastly, changing the country's name from Philippines to Maharlika would transform the land's energy and people back to its authentic nature, honoring indigenous rights and diverse cultural heritage within the seven-plus thousand islands.

DEO PALMA

ABOUT THE AUTHOR

Deo Palma is a dynamic leader and the author of "**Maharlika: In Search of Identity**" and its *'Forthcoming 2nd Edition.'* He is also a collaborative author of the *'Awakening Starseeds' book series Vol. 2 and 3.'*

Deo is the founder of The Confederation of Maharlika Society called **'Ang Kasama,'** advocating the change of a conquered country's name, the Philippines, back to its original natural name, ***'Maharlika.'***

As a spiritual-environmentalist-activist protecting the biodiversity of Maharlika Paradise sanctuary and his headquarter of 'Ang Kasama,' he provides assistance to the indigenous residents, such as medical help and emergency support during devastating typhoons and giant floods in the country. As a protector of human **'LIFE,'** animals, and especially **'children,'** he keep them safe against human trafficking, Deo provided the **'Mahal Foundation'** in Maharlika, serving 7 daycare centers to support the no-income to low-income working Mothers in need of help.

He advocates Universalism and practices Yoga, meditation, and vegetarianism. His spiritual practice led him to self-realization in *'Service to the Universe'* as a social service humanitarian provider and guides others back to their spiritual nature, ecology, and social activism. He traveled thousands of miles across the globe to dedicate his life to uplifting human consciousness through education as an International Meditation and Yoga teacher, teaching the code of ethics to the less fortunate in Africa and Brazil for decades, and now in his Motherland, Maharlika, since 1989 to the present. If you wish to support Deo's projects in Maharlika, here's how to donate via PayPal. Email Deo at: deopalma02@gmail.com

4

TRANSITION FROM DARKNESS TO LIGHT

BY: MAYA THE SHAMAN

Important Timeline - The year 2022

Humanity is about to release many false beliefs and dogmas as we witness world events unfolding! The year 2022 and forward signifies an important timeline in the history of our world to be realized by the awakening of many others, referred to as *"The Mass Awakening or Great Awakening"* The awakened ones already knew that this was an important timeline in our lives and our planet – a moment to witness a cosmic grand-scale drama exposing what's hidden in dark and stagnant places in many areas of our world.

Dreaming of a Beautiful Earth Mother

As I write this, *"It's Full moon in the cool month of May,"* Spring of 2022, when everything around vibrates with the sweet and fresh blossoms of flowers, awakening us from the deep Winter cold months in my Appalachian mountain homestead, which my daughter calls *"The Crystal Mountains.'* My Iris blossom flowers exploded with their deep vibrant blue colors to say I'm back! The plentiful crystal quartz around this land seems to awaken as well. They were pulled out by the roots of the old trees to the surface. A Native American Cherokee Indian told me once that these semi-precious milky white stones in my land are the *'feminine intuitive crystal quartz'* of Mother Earth, carrying historical knowledge and wisdom. *"I reprogrammed them for clarity, protection, and healing."*

Similarly, through meditation, we can reprogram our inner gems and well-being into healing, positivity, magnificence and abundance, so we, too, exude our true Love and Light for this beautiful creation as Co-creators of our dear Mother Earth and the Cosmos. Our planet will be more beautiful when we all care for her as she returns to her original high frequency.

Full Moon Eclipse 2022

This Spring Full Moon on May 16, 2022, is also called 'Flower Full Moon' with a very important message for humanity. It's a beautiful time of the year, yet pockets of chaos and crisis exist in many parts of our world. No need to deny, cover it up or pretend! A relative truth.

I'm not an astrologer, but I like to familiarize myself with zodiac signs to understand humans and our world. Full moons are typically auspicious for rituals, spiritual practices, or celebrations, but this specific full Moon comes with an eclipse in Scorpio. I find it personally significant since my Mother's sign is Scorpio. I have a direct understanding of how it feels to be in the arms of a Scorpio - the loving, spiritual but fierce when directly opposed, or when she believes that something is not in agreement with her! It can be lethal because it is ruled by Pluto, the planet of Life and Death.

The year 2022 is '**fierce.**' With the advent of this full moon eclipse, humanity gets to feel its effect. Many pain points come up yet are transformative as we witness the power to let the energies of the Universe collide in clearing anything on its way. *"Consider it like a big roller steam engine has arrived to flatten the rough and thorny edges within our realities, only to recreate a better roadway for us to tread upon. In the process, others get run over with this super engine, and the ones in the way of cosmic renovation get crushed."*

Beliefs & Dogmas

Our beliefs of all sorts are being tested, and dogmas get a face-to-face confrontation of what is no longer true. 'Lies' are surfacing to be seen as Satya Yuga (Age of Truth) is in preparation to move out of Kali Yuga (the Dark Age) towards the Golden Age to manifest the rightful and highest good for humanity in our world. The intuitive beings are seizing opportunities despite crisis and chaos by taking action to perform Light work – they are the conduit for this massive awakening. Each of us is a part of this momentous shift. We are being asked to clear the weeds around the blooming growth of a beautiful garden we are creating at this time. It asks us to do the work: Internal, inner work, cultivating our authentic personalities, and External, where time takes us to muscle the struggle for clearing our personal space, our home, career, relationships, or being in service to our planet Earth! This inevitable transformation cannot be stopped!

"It gets worse before it gets better!"

So prepare, on all levels, because either we learn to balance the inner and outer aspects of ourselves to go with the Cosmic flow or resist. It will not be the same work for everyone, but it's definitely working time! When we resist change, pain is felt even more! Denials and hiding truth will not work at this time. It will all be exposed. This is the nature of such a transition we as humanity are going through.

It's massive and expansive, but we are getting called upon to use our God-given power to choose the rightful direction and use the power of our hearts and minds to see clearly what is out of alignment and how we can realign back to the Source - Source of ALL that is - Supreme God of this Universe.

Auspicious Full Moon Celebration

Being said, I gather my flowers from my garden and turn them into a bouquet of offerings to join a birthday celebration dedicated to an ascended spiritual Master - Shrii Shrii Anandamurtiji, who was born in this auspicious time. In perspective, Gautama Buddha was born on a full moon as well. The celebration is held at a Yoga Center within walking distance from where I live. I arrived with my offerings and placed them on a 'Puja' table with other assorted flowers offered by the devotees. Offerings are part of the gift-giving grateful expressions towards the Master for his spiritual guidance and blessings to commemorate his coming to Earth. Pictures of the Master and spiritual symbols are displayed too. When sentimental people exhibit photos of their loved ones, it's similar to how spiritual aspirants display photos of their spiritual teachers to show their love and honor for His guidance. The event vibrated with dancing, singing Kiirtan, and group meditation.

Stolen Spiritual Symbols

The puja table was also decorated with a symbol called *'Pratik,'* two triangles meeting together, creating a perfect 6-point star symmetry fused with a rising sun in the middle, and at the very core is a symbol of a swastika which signifies *"Victory to the Light."* On the other hand, Hitler had stolen the swastika symbol from the East, twisted it, and inverted its sacred meaning and intention, then *"From Light to dark, Hitler used this revered symbol to destroy humanity with no shame-no guilt."*

Stolen sacred symbols, words, and contents were stolen, inverted and made famous for satisfying some unoriginal false creator with no good intention but for distorting sacredness. It's like many other false ideas and creations by false creators. As we now know, we live in an inverted false matrix created by false, corrupt leaders from all parts of our world, and like an octopus with tentacles and suction cups ready to take what was not theirs. But *"We, the people,"* are seeing in plain sight how degenerate this world has become. People call these false creators; crooks, goonies, thieves, gangsters, and liars.

Programming & Deprogramming

A lot of what humans have been programmed to believe

comes from those who want to control humanity, including the practice of the 'Dark Arts.' But not for long, because very soon, this inverted timeline and people involved in it are now being hunted by the light warriors. Before this, they chased the light beings using fear tactics. But as we move closer to the ***'Eternal Truth,'*** we become fearless, speak out and take dynamic actions on behalf of claiming back our world from the hands of these crooks.

In my original healing Modality, ***'Infinite Cosmic Records,'*** it is important to recognize and reconcile with what ***'was,'*** before we can shift and move forward to what ***'is'*** would look like. Infinite Cosmic Records holds the past, present and future Cosmic discoveries.

The Advent of the Dark Age

Mother Earth provides us with the grounds we walk on, so we can experience life with her clean water, clean air, and soil for our foods to harvest, but the dark forces add chemicals to our water, chemicals on foods, toxic sprays on the air we breathe, creates multiple wars (large and small), stolen children and humans via human trafficking, and many types of social disruptions affecting our well-being.

To summarize the advent of this dark age, Mother Earth and her children have suffered greatly at the hands of cruel unconscious treatment by those who have no respect and honor for our Earth Mother and all her living beings called **"LIFE."**

Any attempt of goodness has been attacked on all levels, sabotaged on a mass scale. The dark virus spread quickly because some of the poorest populations on Earth were enticed to do crooked things. And just as you may want to know, *'poverty'* is one of the dark agendas because poor people have no resources and are desperate for survival. Therefore they can easily be manipulated, and some turn into criminals. The vital factors for living a sovereign and healthy life for those who sincerely co-existed with Gaia were being destroyed, and our history has been filled with violence. They occupied many governments on our planet and strategically took over the many divisions laid out on the lower parts of the government–infiltrating all the way down to some civilians systematically, from the court of justice, media, banking, large corporations, etc.) "Witch hunt, destruction of the indigenous people, wars, and now our entire planet has been dominated by these crooks."

People who want to live a simple life or advance in any form of growth with Gaia have been blocked. The residents of planet Earth have been robbed of our right to live in peace freely. Our birthrights to experience true happiness and the advancement of authentic spiritual gifts were ridiculed and hampered by the opposing factions and even squashed. The struggle has always been our companion, and threats and fear are the means set in place by dark rulers and minions.

For example, when a Spiritual Master, Shrii Shrii Anandamurtiji, spoke about economic and political reforms as a spiritual way of life to free humanity from exploitation and other fundamental rights of human beings, the President of India, Indira Gandhi, put him in jail, where he fasted for 5 years for the wrong treatment they have done towards him in the early 70s. Then they created 'havoc and fear' by chasing his devotees in India. Shocked and terrified of such sudden events, devotees hid and kept quiet. Those who have realized and dedicated themselves to their Spiritual Master's teaching on humanitarian cause and moral standing fearlessly protested to Free their

Master and publicly self-sacrificed themselves through self-immolations as a sacred protest against injustice.

"Life and Death intertwined."

Similarly, many unknown heroes of today have continued to fight the dark system. *"We, as the people,"* may not know them by names, but they are our heroes who tirelessly devoted their lives in service of the people. We may not even know or cannot comprehend that there are beings so *'good-hearted'* ready to put their lives on the line *'to give others their freedom'* to exist in our timeline. They are on a triumphantly humanitarian mission of removing darkness from Earth. It's been spiritual warfare! Now, *"We, the People"* on our planet can see this!

On the other hand, weak-minded people get possessed by entities and demons who can't make up their minds where to lean. Left in darkness, they get taken over. Black magic is a practice by dark minions called 'Dark Arts,' which put spells on ordinary human beings. They cause 'Negative' situations that persist within humanity in this dark age. As Dark forces gained power, they controlled people, places, and resources everywhere. Yet, the vast majority of humanity simply just wants to live in peace, love, and harmony. The basic necessities of people, security, and safety are important, which were also sabotaged at every step.

Dark Work: Crime Against Humanity

I'd like to share a few examples: During the first year of the *'Pandemic 2019-2020,'* I was in Bali, Indonesia, and Maharlika (the Philippines). The Maharlika workers worldwide lost their jobs in the countries they were working in. Most of them work outside the country as service providers paid month-to-month and have huge responsibilities to take care of their families left behind. And because of this pandemic, they lost their jobs, and coming back home means no earnings and no food for those they support!

I have heard people coming back and committing suicide because the intensity of the lockdown in the Philippines was intolerable with no income. A poor single mother during the earlier lockdown who fed her children hand to mouth struggled to feed her children and went blank-dark from desperation hearing her babies cry from hunger and nothing she could do to feed them - killed her 3 children, killed herself for loss of hope. Then a rich man in the Philippines with a big heart, who could not live with himself seeing his countrymen, women, and children starve, distributed rice and other foods to many places and to many people in the country, but he was locked up in jail for helping people! Tell me, what type of people do these to the suffering humanity? While a doctor who had a clinic that found a cure for Covid has been shut down, and not allowed to practice his God-given skills to help others! Tell me, what soulless people are running the show? **WHO** are these demons? And a friend of mine whose sister is very healthy died immediately from a mandatory vaccine! You may ask, "What kind of a world is this?" ***'It's the world of the Dark Ages and Dark minions!'***

The Dark World is upside down, topsy turvy. Through these ongoing crisis that has been premeditated by the dark forces conquering our world, controlling people, claiming they 'OWN' everything and everyone on this planet, and thinking they can do whatever they want to twist and turn around the Cosmic plan as they desire is no longer accepted – *"This can NO longer continue!"* The Universe has a greater plan for humanity!

Are Monsters Real?

I lived in the midst of Los Angeles, California for a decade. You will find bulletin boards with creepy monster-looking prints all around the City! Dark and negative projections of distorted humans advertised looking like monsters that fed subconscious fears in humans. These images lower human frequency, making humans vulnerable to energetic feeding ground by the dark forces.

'Monsters,' were the words used by Master Anandamurtiji to describe these beings, and Don Pedro, my great-great-grandfather Shaman, said, 'No Mercy' to these creatures because these monsters have *"No respect for Life."* They create fear, energetically feeds on people, want to reduce the populations on Earth, destroys the economy and create their one-world government, claiming each of the countries on Earth their own. Imagine totalitarian control! I can't, and I don't agree!

They believe they have the claim and rights over all the resources, things, and people – disregarding what all humans think or feel. This narcissistic belief caused a huge clash between the bearers of Light against the dark forces. Spiritual war is lit until it's done, yet not everyone can see it. It is happening now. Despite it, the Great Universe does not allow the total destruction of life on Earth at this juncture of spiritual evolution called ascension.

There is Divine intervention, and *"WE, the People,"* no longer tolerate these abusive ways. *"We, the People,"* demand justice and deserve the entrance to our **'Golden Age,'** ascension of values, purifying our bodies and minds, ready to claim back all our natural birth rights to health, sovereignty, abundance, and freedom!

THE TRANSITION PERIOD

- From Darkness to Light -

An inspirational passage from a book by Shrii Shrii Anandamurtiji with a relevant message for humanity called *"The Transition Period."*

*"What does **'Yugasandhi'** mean? 'Yuga' means 'Age,' and 'Sandhi' means 'Joint.' Therefore, 'Yugasandhi' means 'Juncture Before Ages.'*

*At a certain stage in the movement of human society along its path, the behavior, manners, intellect, and wisdom of the people cease to develop - they become static; and society loses its capacity to move forward. This is the critical juncture in history when society feels the need for an extraordinarily powerful personality, a **'Mahasambhuti.'** At this juncture, the advent of such a personality is inevitable.*

*It has been already said that **'Sadvipras'** (light warriors/heroes) will be at the hub of the social cycle to guide and control the movement of the society. They will not allow anyone to perpetuate torture or exploitation. However, at the stage of acute staticity in the society, which occurs every three to four thousand years, a great and extraordinary powerful person's advent is extremely necessary. Such a figure or 'Mahasambhuti' infuses dynamism in the social body and accelerates the speed of movement. All the virtuous people in the world respond to his call and rally around him. He creates a polarization in society: the virtuous versus the wicked. In the clash between the two groups, the virtuous people emerge victorious by dint of their special efforts coupled with the grace of the great personality. His advent itself signifies victory in the war. The mark of victory is sure to be imprinted on the forehead of the virtuous. The brave companions of this*

Mahasambhuti accompany him from age to age, preferring to work with Him than attain their own liberation. They may or may not have great ambitions and may or may not suffer from superiority or inferiority complexes, but no evil element in this world can defeat these blessed people. Rather, in the last phase of the conflict, the evil forces are bound to accept total defeat. Therefore, to those of you marching forward on the path of virtue, the path of Dharma, I say, "Keep marching on safely and without concern."

Shiva's companions were not reputable scholars but were virtuous people who were always ready to fight against sin. In history, they are called ***"Shiva's spiritual soldiers."*** *You should remember that in the present world, you are Shiva's retinue or 'gana.' That is,* ***"You have come to the world for Victory and not for defeat."*** *A few thousand years ago, Krsna was born. At this time also, his companions, the gopas and gopis of Vraja, who worked with him to accelerate the speed of the social movement, were also not profound scholars or learned people, but it was they who were victorious. In those days, many songs were sung praising those great people.*

In the present day, you can see how the social movement is grinding to a halt. When social progress loses its velocity, it is called 'Yugasandhi' (Transition Period). "You have all been born in such a Transitional period and have assembled here today." In the future, the honest and virtuous people of the society will respond to Your call and will unite. The same polarization is taking place now as it occurred in the past: the honest people are with you and will remain with you; the dishonest people will oppose you now and will continue their efforts to block your progress in the future. "You will surely be victorious whenever there's a war between 'Dharma' (human purpose) and 'Adarma' (against human purpose)." You are not alone - Dharma is with you, the benevolent intellect is with you, and I am also with you.

—Shrii Shrii Anandamurti, December 30, 1978, Published in Ananda Vacanamrtam Part 7

Humanity is Moving Forward

It is the first time in the history of our planet, in my lifetime, that our entire world is experiencing a crisis at all levels of our lives in all countries! Human beings have got to experience the worst before it gets better on a mass level, to scale up the shift that is about to take place on Earth. It's weighing up the dark and light within the cosmic scale. Those who have created karmic suffering for humanity have a severe karmic debt to pay with huge interests. It's massive, and behind it, humanity is not alone in this struggle. For the essence of struggle will soon be revealed. In other collaborative books, I was a part of, I have mentioned that the *"Darkest hour is before the light."* An individual's goal is to work on themselves depending upon the areas of life where something is out of balance. It can be physical, mental, emotional, or spiritual. This is the time to look at one's individual creation and fix what has gone wrong, and *"Be a part of the Light movement that awakens us."* As you awaken, and harness your courage — free from fear, you contribute to the greater good of humanity and the higher frequency on Earth and the 'Age of Truth' becomes our new reality.

With this message from an ascended Master, I hope you are inspired as I am. *"The future is brighter than you can ever imagine!" Says* Shrii Shrii Anandamurtiji. ***Let's move into the wondrous Golden Age, and Claim Victory to the Light!***

Salamat Po,

~Maya The Shaman

~

SAYING:

"One who does all work as an offering to God — abandoning selfish attachment to results — remains untouched by Karmic reaction or sin as a lotus leaf never gets wet by water. "

—Bhagavad Gita, 5.10

MAYA VERZONILLA, AKA MAYA THE SHAMAN

ABOUT THE AUTHOR

Maya The Shaman, Energy Healer, Shaman, Multimedia artist and Author of several collaborative books.

Maya is the original Creatrix of the healing modalities: **Lemurian Code Healing & Infinite Cosmic Records**, providing Shamanic Lemurian Energy healing, Spiritual life coaching, and teaching.

She co-authored several collaborative books, including the Awakening Starseeds series, Pillars of Light, and the Amazon bestseller Energy Healing & Soul Medicine book. Maya shares her sovereign voice as an authentic storyteller and educator to convey her spiritual message to the world and uses her freedom of expression to stay on relevant topics to our time while honoring her ancestors and lineage as a descendant of the ancient land of Mu, while serving her Dharma with the world.

Her forthcoming books are *"Infinite Cosmic Records: Sacred Doorways to Healing and Remembering" and "Descendants of Lemuria."* In contribution to transformation, Maya shares her visions and wisdom in documentary films called *'Guns, Bombs, War: A Love Story'* and *'The Cure'* by Hollywood's French Director Emmanuel Itier, Produced by Actress Sharon Stone.

See what clients say about Maya and her work. Visit California's LA magazine interview on *the 'Infinite Cosmic Records'* modality. Copy and paste this link to your browser: ***Maya Verzonilla, AKA Maya the Shaman | Formidable Woman Magazine.***

For More Info, go to:
www.MayaTheShaman.com

5

WAY OF THE STARSEED

BY: LESLIE ALLYN FINKEL

Remembering My Truth

"It was night and somewhere in the middle of the ocean. I'm in a small rowboat when suddenly I fall into the waves. I'm falling, falling, spiraling as I go down into the deep dark water. I was scared at first, but strangely, I could still breathe. I keep tumbling deeper and deeper through the darkness. I realize I'm not drowning. Eventually, I find myself landing softly on the sandy bottom of the ocean floor. It is completely light, and I start walking. I feel at home."

I had this recurring dream, not just once or twice. I dreamt of it dozens of times, starting when I was three years young and well into my twenties. I became excited about the adventure I was about to have whenever the dream would return. I was never afraid of dying. I looked forward to my fun stroll on the bottom of the ocean. Go figure that two of my favorite TV shows in the 70s were *Voyage To The Bottom Of The Sea* and *Flipper.*

I first heard of Atlantis and Lemuria in my twenties. But it was not until my forties that I discovered they were not just fantasy stories. I have many friends who have past life memories of living in one of those places. I didn't. Or so I thought. It has been suggested to me by several seers that this recurring dream is a memory of my becoming a Dolphin Being when Atlantis sank underwater. I chose to stay with the people to help and protect them in the face of catastrophe. This decision ties directly into the core of my Being. 'Abandon ship' was never an option. Perhaps this explains why I have webbed toes? Yes, I actually have webbed toes.

Dolphins have an inexplicable affinity for humans. There have been countless times when they saved or protected people in the oceans, whether from shark attacks or having fallen overboard. Researchers at Melbourne University recently conducted a study into the human DNA and that of marine mammals. They determined that dolphins are the closest ancestors to us humans. "No matter how weird it may appear, dolphins used to have two legs and a couple of arms in place of fins. They lived side by side with the people," says Dr. Leslie Huskerway, a lead biologist. Coincidently, dolphins may have parted company with Homo Sapiens some 250,000 years ago. This discovery collaborates with the Mayan calendar, which spans over 260,000 years and ties back to Atlantis.

Echoes of Past or Future Lives

I can recall every vivid dream I've ever had, even when I was only two years young. In one of my favorite dreams, I was the commander of a spherical space colony vessel. It had dozens of levels with societies comprised of many different types of people —humans only. You might say, sure, you must have watched *Star*

Trek. Well, a fact about this dream I think will make you reconsider is I dreamt this long before seeing *Star Trek* or any other sci-fi movie. I was only five years young when this dream happened nightly for six or seven days straight. Each night I tapped into it and started right where I had left off the previous morning.

My dad worked in the aerospace industry in the 1960s. He brought freeze-dried astronaut food home, such as powdered ribeye. You added water to reconstitute it. It tasted horrible. Then there was 'Tang,' an orange-flavored drink for U.S. astronauts—not bad. He also brought home huge color laminated photos of the Earth, moon, and lunar spacecraft. Did these items awaken memories of my past or even future lives? An interesting thought.

In 2011, I traveled to Italy with my wife, Sabine Messner, also featured in this book. We attended a mastermind retreat at Mona Lisa's country home in Tuscany with a group of highly talented women from all around the world. I was the lucky guy who got to be the 'Protector' wherever we went. One evening, we all sat beside a glowing fire under the night sky and told stories about our lives. I spoke about how I had a heart attack at only age thirty-nine. It made no sense to me when it happened because I played multiple sports in the Police Olympics and was a runner and powerlifter.

While I was describing the incident, one of the women suddenly jumped up and said she had a past life vision of me. She had this extraordinary ability to touch a wall or physical object and see past events, like a movie scene playing in front of her eyes. She said she saw me when I was an Amazonian. An enemy started to attack us, so I told the other women to run while I stayed and held them back. She said, *"You saved all the women with your heroic actions but were tragically stabbed in the heart by a sword."* Upon hearing her vision, I instantly started tearing up. I knew it was true beyond any shadow of a doubt. I've not fared well in other past lives too. I've been told I died in many battles.

Soul Frequencies

Remember back in kindergarten when the teacher asked all the children to raise their hand if they thought they were a Starseed? Ya right. I don't remember that either. I just remember not understanding why the other kids behaved the way they did. Why were there always physical and verbal bullies teasing and picking on shy and vulnerable kids? I didn't get it. I still don't get it. Neither my quizzical lack of understanding nor unwavering protector instinct and sense of justice ever faded away—not in any grade nor at any age, and not even during my career when I stood up for my colleagues. I always acted fiercely heartfelt. It wasn't a choice. I *had* to listen to my heart.

I remember growing up wanting to protect other children. When I was only four, a neighbor boy was chasing my older brother around and around a car while wielding a pocket knife. I ran to the boy's house and pounded on the door to tell his mom. She came out and stopped her son from stabbing my brother. Almost any brother would have done the same thing, but it sets the tone for my life.

One day when I was in second grade, my class received a visit from the special education class with developmentally challenged children and adults. They had made lasagna for the entire school and were going from classroom to classroom to share it. Every kid in my class hemmed and hawed at the idea of touching their food. I felt embarrassed for my classmates and didn't understand their cruel behavior, nor did I let it stop me from graciously enjoying some really awesome lasagna.

I've had many other experiences where I felt a calling to stand up for children or adults in need. The last one I'll leave you with is how I created a charity event to benefit the Arizona Special Olympics, which I ran for nine years. I raised tens of thousands of dollars, enabling special needs athletes to train, travel and compete year-round. I named it "Law Enforcement Torch Run Charity Car Show & Barbecue." My LETR charity not only benefited the athletes, it brought local communities, families, and law enforcement together in a caring way. One of my favorite recollections is of a young little leaguer in uniform marveling at a classic yellow 1950s Chevy with a shiny chrome engine, and a huge Tweety Bird painted on the underhood. One of the countless moments that still bring a smile to my face.

I have always been the protector and defender in this lifetime and many others. I have been a martial artist since I was a teenager. I trained to prevent fights from ever starting. Yet, I was always ready and able to defend myself, my loved ones, friends, or strangers in need. I love to help others rise when they're down, to be that helping hand.

Multi-Dimensional Soul Journeys

I participated in three guided multi-dimensional Soul Journeys that my wife Sabine facilitated. The landscapes I traversed during these journeys were just as vivid and real as the memory of my last vacation. These journeys reestablished important archetypal parts of myself that were scattered and forgotten in the 3D Matrix.

On the first journey, I find myself sitting on top of a mountain peak, overlooking other mountains when I feel a presence. Through my mind's eye, I see a bearded man with long curly hair come up behind me. He is wearing denim pants and a flannel shirt and looks like he is in his thirties. He reaches down and gently pulls me up by my hand. As I stand up, he smiles and says, "It's Time To Go To Work." I know this is God. After this journey, I was ready to fully live my Soul purpose, which I call Unstoppable Healing™.

On the second journey, I am walking on a trail in the woods. I come to a simple wooden gate. I unlatch it, and it swings open. I continue my journey until I come to a sunny yet shady spot. There's a stream flowing, making a lovely sound. A beautiful white stallion comes galloping up. I see it. But it is me. I am the stallion. Next, I trot to a new Soul plane where I am that horse on the mountain top. A big bird, condor, or eagle flies to me. It says, "Love Everyone You Meet." I gallop down the mountain to the beach—bright, sunny, beautiful sand. I see my human feet in the sand. I dig them in. I am still the horse. A sea turtle appears and says, "There Are No Accidents." Years later, my Akashic and Mayan Cosmology readings echo that I am the Centaur, the condor, and the wise turtle all rolled into one.

On the third journey, I'm wearing a spacesuit, about to jump through a clear shute inside a transparent space vehicle and down to the Earth. Just as I'm ready to leap, God pulls me aside and says, *"Only You Decide What You Are."*

"Dreaming Into the Future" is about remembering where we came from and who and what we are so we can play our best part in shaping the future. I freely share fragments of my life, stories, memories, dreams, recollections, and feelings with you. My goal here is to illustrate that we all have many puzzle pieces we need to sift through and carefully piece together for our Souls to become whole once again. The hardest part is sometimes these puzzle pieces aren't easily discernible, nor do they necessarily appear all at once.

Our Original Soul Incarnation

We all originate from Source, God, the Creator, or whatever name you prefer. I believe God chooses the location in the vast universe to best support our first Soul incarnation based on what we choose to express as our Soul essence. This galactic birthplace sets our Soul's blueprint and forms the overall theme for our many lives—past, present, and future.

When I had my first Akashic Record reading, I learned that my Soul's original incarnation was in our closest stellar neighborhood—the Alpha Centauri system. It consists of three stars named Alpha Centauri A, Alpha Centauri B, and Proxima Centauri. This star system lies just over four light-years away. That's about 25 trillion miles or 38 trillion km. Alpha Centaurians are known for being protectors and defenders of truth and justice. Their mission is to serve and advance societies through knowledge and technology. They are highly advanced, practical problem solvers who feel a duty to help others.

In a more recent Akashic Record reading from 2022, I learned that I trained as a warrior in the star system 'Hercles' (Greek name before Romans changed it to Hercules). I also discovered I trained as a Greek Olympian, not just in sports but in mystery schools. Isn't it interesting that I ran track and threw the discus, shot put, and javelin in high school and the Police Olympics as an adult? In 2010, when my wife and I traveled throughout the Mediterranean, we spent some time in Greece, not only at the temples of the Gods but at the Olympiad, where she filmed me going through the motions of throwing the discus, shot put, and javelin. No wonder I felt so at home.

Most importantly, I received a clear message in my reading that I'm here to raise people's frequencies higher in preparation for living in the Aquarian age. To change the frequency of battle altogether, ending the external "battlefield" of arrows, spears, bullets, and bombs and addressing our internal conflicts and struggles with traumatic memories and energies instead. We rapidly restore and reestablish peace from the inside out through quantum healing, integration, and knowledge.

Way To The Future

I've been immersed in the world of technology for a long time—more than 31 years, mainly as a computer operating systems specialist. I spent two years as a civilian at System Development Corp working on U.S. Air Force Satellite Control, three years as a software engineer at Burroughs/Unisys Corp, and 26 years in charge of mission-critical IT systems at the City of Phoenix Police, for the fifth largest city in the United States. My formal education in modern technology came full circle when I trained in a five-thousand-year-old healing modality with one of the world's leading teachers of Chi Nei Tsang—Thubten Khadro, a Tibetan Dakini. I use this 'ancient technology' in my Unstoppable Healing practice to reboot and revitalize people's bodies and emotional states.

My way to the future is as a Quantum Healer working with the interconnected systems of the body, mind, and Soul. The Fascia system is a multi-dimensional web that connects directly to the morphogenetic field. By working in this sacred way and witnessing our incredible human self-healing capabilities, I see how truly advanced we are, even when we think we are broken.

As a Projector in the Human Design System, I'm a natural guide, here to light the way for others. I take my clients on a subconscious journey into their bodies while holding a lantern so they can see what they need to see and process. Together we focus on their "Internal battlefield" so they can skip 'trying to figure out' what's causing their physical and emotional hurt and go directly to the unfiltered source—their body. As their 'bodyguard,' I ensure they finally feel safe accessing and permanently releasing old, stored traumatic energies and emotions, some even from past lives and lineage. As they become unencumbered from pain and strife, they move forward in living their purpose with clarity and zest.

For the past decade, I have worked hands-on with hundreds of clients. I am excited to incorporate new quantum modalities, frequency technologies, and other energy tools into my practice, enabling me to work with clients remotely, no matter where they live.

I invite you to join my Unstoppable Healing Starseed community, dive deeper into your own Unstoppable Healing, discover how you can remember your true self, and determine your future way. Receive your welcome gift, book your Unstoppable Healing sessions, arrange your private multi-day healing retreat, get helpful resources, plus enjoy an extended photo album of my fantastic and fun Starseed Remembrance Journey! Join us at UnstoppableHealing.

~

SAYING:

"Love one another and help others to rise to the higher levels, simply by pouring out love. Love is infectious and the greatest healing energy."

— Sai Baba

LESLIE ALLYN FINKEL

ABOUT THE AUTHOR

Leslie Allyn Finkel is on a mission to free people from their traumas, pains, and everyday stresses so they can thrive and enjoy life to their fullest. He is the Founder of Unstoppable Healing™, where he leads clients to profound life and health changes using an ancient Taoist healing science called Chi Nei Tsang.

Leslie is passionate about helping people heal holistically from the inside out. His clients report astounding results, including relieving chronic pain from accidents and physical injuries, releasing emotional traumas and anxieties, or eliminating digestive and hormonal issues.

Leslie enjoyed a 31-year career in Information Technology. He devoted 26 years to the City of Phoenix Police, where he proudly administered all mission-critical systems, including the 911 Emergency System.

He has a Bachelor in Mathematics and Computer Science from Tulane University and 25 combined years studying Chi Nei Tsang, Tai Chi, and Martial Arts. He is a co-author of the Amazon-Bestseller book Energy Healing & Soul Medicine: Stories of Healing & Miracles.

Join us at: UnstoppableHealing.com/StarseedWay.

6

NAVIGATING THE 4TH DIMENSION

BY: SABINE MESSNER

The Darkening of The Light

"Only in the darkness can you see the stars."

— Dr. Martin Luther King Jr.

Here we are at the edge of the world as we know it.

Titans of old thundering in the skies like tornados. The bedrock of thoroughly established reality is rumbling, crumbling, gushing open. Century-old belief systems are falling apart like rubble below our feet, pulverized into vanishing dust. A thousand shades of greyish lies, like ghosts, engulfing millions of Souls in smoke screen mirrors into infinity. Shiny spells casting civilizations into the ultimate dissolution of all illusions.

As if we hadn't had enough.

But no, there's more kool-aid to drink from this grand unleashing fire hose. Every day, like clockwork, another globally orchestrated agenda swarm is released. More bad news, more white noise, and plenty of nonsense to make everyone dizzy. The failure of this system. The collapse of that sector. The cataclysmic decline of that country. The destruction of that nation. Global communities get stirred around from this side to that angle and back around, immerged into a collective soup of distraction, exhaustion, fear, and worry—the perfect recipe for one disaster compounding onto another. We've all been prepared for this all-too-familiar doomsday scenario. It's a strange, eerie relief. Sweet surrender into the 'inevitable.' Let this never-ending Matrix nightmare we've all grown tired of be finally done in one big bang as it began.

Algorithms come to the rescue, monitoring from all directions, medicating mental upsets, and sanitizing our every thought with kindness. Artificial sky nets measure every footprint. After all, we are the Carbon Humans—polluters, destroyers of this Earth plane, which must be saved from ourselves. Quantum computers power the new Meta Verse, shuffling well-meaning people like herds into virtual safe-havens. For your safety and security and the survival of our planet, let us imprint and imprison you so we can control your destiny and that of your children as we cultivate their optimal rainbow reproduction inside our virtual Petri dishes.

Nothing left untouched. Nothing left sacred.

Every single living thing 'uploaded' into 0s and 1s. Chipped, traced, tracked, and bar-coded—like animals trapped in breeding factories or zoos. Like vegetables "Rounded-Up" in robotized greenhouse farms and turned into patented GMO crops. Why would the greed that rules the world stop at our front doors? Notification sounds of hell turn into synthetic smelter fumes. Star seeds torched in the sight of unspeakable untruths, burning up in flames, incinerating infinite layers of separation and distortion. Excruciating torture. It's the AI inferno of the Soul.

Until that exquisite moment when it all becomes still and quiet. When we remember who we are and why we are here. As the Earth's crust is cracking from all the fracking, so is our shell of protection. Scorched a million-fold, we turn to titanium. Our core is untouchable. As the world is disintegrating, we are reintegrating.

Starseeds, locked and loaded.

Born from the ashes, we did not come here to go up in flames. We did not train for thousands of lifetimes to sell our Soul—the most precious asset of all there is and will ever be. And by God, we did not come to buy into the same-old stories. Oh no. We came to see. And see it all the way through. First, we ache, then we arc. We receive revelations our loved ones can't conceive. Like vessels of Love, we hold archetypal space for the rebirth of the Crystalline Humans. We originate from Love. We come from Source.

We are the Arcs, archetypal liberators—dancing with swirling timelines at the brink of the abyss. We are the Arcs, chain breakers of enslavement— lifting bedrocks of fear and oppression. We are the Arcs, realm bridgers to the Golden Age —anchoring humanity's highest trajectory. We are the Arcs, eternal angelic torch bearers—igniting each other's flames.

We're coming home. And we're coming in hot.

Graduating from the 3rd Dimension

"In a world where you can do anything, cut yourself some slack."

Welcome on board the Arc—our 5th-dimensional Earth-ship, Angel!

Congratulations, you broke through a vibrational light barrier of tectonic proportions. This frequency threshold, which we lovingly call the 'terror crust,' holds generations of your lineage in checkmate. But not you. On Dr. David Hawkins' Scale of Consciousness, you surpassed 100— the frequency of fear. You broke the chain and can now withstand massive amounts of emotional manipulation (frequency 50). It takes tremendous willpower to stand your ground in a crowd of thousands and not collapse under peer pressure. Well done.

It's a considerable achievement, especially during these end-game times, yet these trying times push us past our limits. The 3rd dimension is where external influences, including well-meaning loved ones, determine what you can and cannot do. This fight-flight conditioning is so deep—it's systemic (frequency range of 20 shame to 150 anger out of 1,000+). It's the root of human suffering. We ordinarily don't have 'the luxury' to question it. We're too busy getting by. Yet, it's emotional warfare inside our body cells. It's like constantly running into an electric fence to the point where you're giving in, giving up, and going numb. That's how multi-generational bondage predicts your destiny as if it's already written in stone.

Yet, you've gone even further, Angel. Reached for more, strived for more, and channeled your grief, dreams, desires, and divine frustration into inspired action. You broke through the ultimate shadow player light barrier. You are the glitch in the Matrix. You made it past 200—the frequency of courage. With its cycles of shame, blame, fear, anger, pride, and competition, the victim-victor game is now a clearly identifiable pattern of your past. You reclaimed ownership of your emotional chemistry and, as such, are finally in the driver seat of your body vehicle.

Now that you have reached a new level in the Game of Consciousness, it's time to buckle up. If you thought freeing yourself from emotional shackles was hard, think again. As a 5D Earth-ship Arc, we still have to navigate fascinating water worlds. Let's get you ready for the tests, trials, and tribulations of the 4th dimension—the vibrational domain of the Mind. Shall we?

Age of Beliefs, Illusion, and Deception

"Lose your Mind to get to your Senses."

Angel, we see such fundamental changes in our reality because of the "Changing of the Guards" on a planetary scale. We are exiting the astrological Age of Pisces, which started around 200 BC, and are entering the Age of Aquarius. These astrological ages have a 2,160-year duration, and the transit passage between them lasts 100-200 years.

While there is no specific end or start date, we can all agree that as of 2020—the year when hindsight became foresight, we're dealing with dramatically different energies. This, my dear Angel, is the Aquarian Age knocking at your door. Forget going back to the old normal. The past is officially over, done, finished, finito. For better or worse, it served its purpose. Now the entire Milky Way is moving on to its next chapter. In just a few short years, we will not recognize the "Brave New World." And brave, we shall and must remain.

If we are to summarize the last 2,160 years that constitute the Piscean Age, we could say it was all about 'programming' the Human Mind to operate in duality. Establish inferiority and superiority in essentially every single aspect of our lives. This duality maintains the hierarchy from top to bottom. The key was to cement opposing belief systems so firmly into our heads that they became foundational, absolute, and unquestionable. Beliefs create reality, and conflicts make the world go round. The black-white chess board—good-bad, left-right, up-down, rich-poor, first-world-third-world. Flip-invert. Rinse-repeat. It's a closed loop, which is why history repeats itself, and the future is entirely predictable.

To innerstand our systematic "belief system conditioning" even further, we need to take a closer look at Neptune. This planet governed the Age of Pisces since it rules its zodiac sign. Neptune is linked to Poseidon, the Greek God of The Sea and ruler of the water world. Remember that algae-haired titan rising from the bottom of the ocean on a chariot with his trident? Yup, that guy.

Neptune is the pathway between divinity and deception. Imagine looking into a deep body of water, such as a lake, and seeing from the surface all the way to the bottom—filtering divine sunlight through all the layers. Now imagine you can only see a few feet of clear water. The deeper you go, the murkier it gets until you reach the slimiest swamp, swarming with gnarly creatures who have never seen the light of day—certainly not in eons. That's Neptune's water world for you. It represents the collective Human Psyche. Neptune is also the gateway to multi-dimensionality. And this is where it gets tricky.

This Poseidon stuff might not be some ancient, far-away myth. You, my Angel, are that Body of water. Our bodies are 80% water, while our brains are even 90% water. Are you aware that you're growing hair and fingernails or that your heart is beating and keeping you alive as you read this chapter? We all have subconscious and unconscious Minds. We spend one-third of our time sleeping in bed and two-thirds sleepwalking through life. Do we really know what's happening in our dream worlds? Could a part of our consciousness live a life in a parallel universe? It makes one wonder what else could be happening in the vast universe of our very own consciousness.

In astrology, Neptune is commonly associated with belief systems and religions. But also con-artistry, insider-trading, illusion, delusion, fabrication, fantasy, and fakery—essentially the entire domain of lies, half-truths, and misinformation we're drowning in. From spirituality to false gurus, from education to mass manipulation, from TV (tell-a-vision) and social media to hypnosis and psychosis. Think of all the books, comics, video games, and movies we've consumed throughout our lives and put into our minds. Good, bad, or ugly, it's all a form of mind programming. It's notoriously difficult to discern with Neptune, and there's always a twist at every turn. What do we truly know versus what we've been told? And what's been hidden from us? If the graduation from the 3rd dimension was about breaking the chains of emotional bondage, the graduation from the 4th dimension is about breaking the chains of mental and illusional entrapment.

The Dawn of the Aquarian Age

"There will come a time when you believe everything is finished. That will be the beginning."

Each astrological age has a planet that oversees this multi-thousand-year evolutionary passage. The governing planet sets the tone, the goals, and how the next chapter will unfold. As you know, we're in the process of moving into the Age of Aquarius, which will be governed by the outer authority planet Uranus, ruler of the zodiac sign Aquarius. In Greek mythology, Uranus was associated with the "personification of heaven"—the primordial Sky God who mated with Gaia, our Mother Earth. According to legend, Uranus is the father of the first generation of titans, including Cronos, later known as Saturn. He is also the grandfather of Neptune and Jupiter. Uranus represents cosmic consciousness, radical awakening, and revolutionary advancement—hence the Great Awakening.

Whereas the Piscean Age was about hierarchy and establishment, the Aquarian Age will make dynamic evolution the new norm. Uranus rattles us from barely waking to gobble up the 4D revelation juice. Trying to outsmart yourself in the 4th dimension based on assumptions and indoctrinations from the old Piscean 3D is a sure-fire mind-trap. The 'new reality' is that we can't think ourselves into the future. Overthinking will loop us right back to where we started. It's also not wise to sit on the fence—hedging and waiting for the other shoe to drop. Be proactive instead of passive. Don't just watch the movie. Be the director of your reality. Remember, Uranus is the Great Awakener, rewarding the 5D pioneers, risk-takers, and innovators.

But fasten your seat belt, Angel. Uranus has a short fuse. He is extremely future-forward and loves to recycle stagnant old paradigm energy to reshape our world. Uranus brings dramatic bursts in consciousness, mind-bending innovations, and unpredictable, even erratic events and changes. Uranus gives rise to rebellion and liberation, but in its worst case, also eccentric dictatorship. We could get free energy and end all forms of greed, extortion, and enslavement. Or we could be ushered into an omni-controlling AI simulation that will blow our circuits.

The key to working with Uranus is to lead with Soul, period.

The Soul's domain starts with the baseline of Love—frequency of 500 on the Hawkins' Scale of Consciousness.

Enlightenment begins at 700 and goes beyond 1,000 into infinity. Your Soul connects you with your Higher Self and gives you direct access to God, Source, Creator, and Great Spirit—whatever name you choose. It brings you clarity, protection, purpose, courage, strength, and synchronicity—all of which you will need. When you lead with Soul, you automatically come from your 5th-dimensional knowing, intuition, and guidance. As soon as you put your Soul in the driver seat of your entire life, your little ego-mind can no longer run the proverbial show, going around in circles, "like a broken record." Stop trying to "figure it out." The way forward is about transfiguration from the inside out. It is the exodus from the logic-based left brain into your "Right Mind" and from there into true unification. "Soul Singularity" versus artificial singularity.

It's high time to get to higher grounds, Angel. Let's talk about 5D.

5th Dimensional Creator Souls

"You are not a drop in the ocean. You are the entire ocean in a drop."
- Rumi

There is a vast space between the particles. This vastness is far more gravitationally powerful than all solid structures in the universe. It contains the very breath of life—the sun, the stars, the planets of the Milky Way, as well as our innate galactic signatures. In quantum physics, this space is called wave potentiality. It's the pure potential where the mystery of life originates —the "All There Is." It's the quantum field for us Arcs to ignite our highest dreams and call in a glorious, prosperous, liberated, and peaceful world to return to this planet. Angel, will you step into this void and make your highest future a reality? Every single vibrationally uplifted 5D Soul is a huge pebble in the great vastness and counts a million-fold. Each Arc is an integral puzzle piece. We are all affected in the unified, morphogenetic field if you hold yourself back or stay stuck. Vice versa, every Arc who advances propels others forward too. We're all in this together, which brings us to my role in the Great Awakening.

I'm a Timeline Keeper. My genius is anchoring Souls in their highest timeline trajectory. I have always known that if I liberate only one Soul, we shift entire lineages and universes. That's why I love connecting individuals, young adults, and even family constellations with their greater purpose using my multidimensional Soul Sight combined with Human Design and Gene Keys. Freeing people from the 3D Matrix and continuously launching divinely inspired entrepreneurs by the hundreds is even closer to my heart. We achieve this by anchoring their Soul blueprint in their brand and expert platform. I coined my spiritual embodiment and financial liberation process, Soul Purpose Branding® and Soul Purpose Wealth™. This is my life's work.

Dear Starseed Angel, we've reached the end of this chapter yet barely scratched the surface. I invite you to learn more about the Age of Aquarius and the critical role you play. Get access to my advanced masterclasses, including "Dimensions of Consciousness," insights on the Tesseract—the wormhole architecture of the 4th dimension, "5D Soul Purpose Wealth Activations," and business and branding guidance for New Paradigm influencers. Plus, exclusive invitations to Starseed retreats and co-creation opportunities.

If there ever was a destiny call in the perhaps thousands or millions of your incarnations, this is it, Angel. Fly with us.

SABINE MESSNER

ABOUT THE AUTHOR

Sabine Messner is a visionary Futurist and 5D Mentor, empowering awakening leaders to be in business with their sacred calling. Combining her Soul Purpose Branding® approach with epigenetic Human Design, Gene Keys, and cutting-edge business and marketing guidance, Sabine helps her clients thrive as divinely-inspired entrepreneurial stewards of the New Earth.

An award-winning Wired Magazine designer, she blends 30+ years in arts, visual communication, and marketing with her extensive studies of quantum healing and indigenous, cross-cultural energy modalities. Sabine's approach is equally enlightening and down-to-earth.

Her latest book collaboration is "Stop Overworking And Start Overflowing - 25 Ways To Transform Your Life Using Human Design." Sabine holds an M.A. in Visual Communication from the Berlin University of the Arts and is the founder of Soul Purpose Branding® and Soul Purpose Wealth™.

Join her at: SoulPurposeWealth.com/AwakeningStarseeds.

7

THE HOLISTIC TRAINER

BY: MICHAEL BARRIOS

"We usually will find our edges, before we find our center."

It took a pandemic to force us to see the imbalances in our lives. Some people gave into the chaos, allowing the fear to cause more disharmony in the body, mind, and spirit. Others began to look inward and onward, seeing that they needed change in their lives. More people started to awaken to the idea that health is multifaceted and it's not just about looking fit. Health is more about feeling balanced. Do you feel mentally well? How do you handle your emotions? Can you move with ease, and do you feel strong? Do you have faith in something or someone larger than yourself? This holistic lens isn't something new but as old as the cosmos. The interconnectedness of everything and everyone creates a whole.

More people are starting to see that we were taught what to think and how to think. We can call it programming. We know this deep down inside. Our souls long for our unique expression. Our beliefs aren't our beliefs but what we collected from our caretakers, teachers, friends, politicians, religious leaders, etc. Many of us are in pain, depressed, and anxious because we aren't making choices that align with who we truly are. We are working off the programming to get us to live lives that aren't ours. I see a world where we choose from the heart, asking our soul for guidance rather than our phones. I see a world where we grow our own foods and know that we have this innate healing system we call our body. We view our bodies as the most cutting-edge technology and that we aren't scared of disease or viruses, but we know that we can overcome anything with quality food, the right amount of movement for ourselves, breathing intentionally, quality water, quality sleep, and managing our thoughts. Energy healing is more common than pharmaceuticals. Tai chi, Qigong, and Yoga are practiced in all schools. Our kids are taught to love our bodies' innate wisdom rather than fear it. The mental disease will be viewed as a spiritual disease, and we will turn to the wisdom and guidance of our ancestors and elders.

The health and wellness industry uses terms like ancestral diet or ancestral wisdom. And it is strongly advised to go outside in nature and *'ground'* yourself on the Earth to help aid with hormonal imbalances and inflammation. Red light therapy, cold plunges, and saunas help push toxins that accumulate and contribute to chronic dis-ease and illness. We work with our bodies' systems to create harmony in our body's ecosystems. We are looking into healing naturally rather than using synthetics or genetically modified products. We are starting to shift our minds back into our bodies through embodiment practices. We are starting to awaken to see how our bodies feel, rather than pushing through the pain or numbing ourselves.

In my practice as a Holistic Practitioner, I see so many

disconnected people from their bodies and spirit. I help people get to the root cause of their pain and not just address the symptoms as most western practices do. If we become more embodied, we can choose our thoughts. Our thoughts create our reality. Our inner world becomes our outer world, our perspective, our reality. Not knowing that their lifestyle choices are the root cause of their injury, illness, or pain. I ask my clients, *"How are you feeling?"* And then, *"How is your body feeling?"*. We must become present to feel both. Often our minds are fixated on our past, which leads to depression or worrying about our future, which makes us anxious. Rarely do I have a client that is present in their body. I find that movement with intention helps my clients become present in their bodies. Feeling the imbalances or the *'tightness'* in specific areas. They didn't realize these sensations before. They push through the pain and do not enjoy the workout, but they get hooked on the marketing or see the results on someone else. They are doing something not because they truly want to or enjoy it, but because there is an aspect of themselves that they do not love. They are going against their own body, giving it the message that, *"You're not enough."* But when we do something wholeheartedly, the body's innate wisdom will work with us. The body always wants to be balanced, and it wants to be in harmony, just like mother nature. We are mother nature. We are sick, overweight, and sad because we go against what mother nature intended. Our bodies are speaking to us, and we have to listen. Low sex drive? Is it the lack of sleep, the processed food, or working a job that you hate? In a toxic relationship? Consistent negative thoughts? When we listen to our bodies and have a training plan that we truly enjoy, our bodies will transform faster than we can imagine. Working smarter, not harder, is the key.

Our bodies will tell us that we are out of balance through

sensation. For most of my clients who see me for hormonal imbalance, depression, losing weight, or rehabbing an injury, it's a simple fix. Quality food, quality water, quality sleep, a balanced movement practice *'working in'* as much as working out, breathing, and addressing limiting beliefs. Through six foundational principles, I coach all my clients and have seen amazing miracles happen.

"We see things not as they are, but as we are."

I've found to be true that many of my clients, myself included, are reacting to emotions versus responding. Emotions are not good or bad. Emotions are energy-in-motion. We can allow it to flow through us, or we can suppress them or repress them. We become a pressure cooker, waiting to release or explode. We need to release this pressure before we explode or implode. We usually regret it when we explode on our family, friends, or work. So we need to express ourselves. Speak our truths and show our unique selves. I use the breath to help my clients express these stuck emotions in the body. Sometimes we call it trauma, or we can call it memories stuck in the body. Our mind can forget traumatic events, but the body does not. Psychologist, physician, and author Gabor Maté states, *"Trauma is not what happens to you; it's what happens inside of you as a result of what happened to you."* It is a subjective experience. What is traumatic to one person might not be traumatic to another. The actual *'trauma'* is the response from within our being during the event. It is a *'trauma response.'* Through somatic release breath-work, the client may be able to release trauma from the body and finally rid themselves of their trauma response. There are several ways in which we as individuals can repattern ourselves, and Somatic release allows the nervous system to start to calm down to begin our true healing process back to balance. Some clients have mentioned that one session of somatic release breath-work feels like years of talk therapy, there was so much emotional release and the felt so clear. Once we clear the body, we clear the mind. Motivation to change our negative patterns becomes easier. We pulled out the roots of the weeds in our garden.

"Be the change you want to see in the world."

I hope to help as many trainers and coaches heal our wounds and integrate our life lessons so we can effectively help our clients achieve their goals and ultimately change the world. If we are not working on loving all aspects of ourselves, we will be blind to the patterns that are hurting us and others around us. We are perfect, but there is still work to heal any pain and fear. Energy healing and many other modalities have helped me release so much of the pain I held on to from past lives, generational trauma, and my current life. I saw how this was affecting my work and my relationships. Understanding the value of knowing how chakras affect not only the mental-emotional aspects of a person but the biological and physiological parts of the body has been so instrumental in my coaching style. Seeing that a foot or knee injury isn't just a physical injury but an energetic injury that will keep occurring until we find out the root cause. For this particular issue, we look to the root chakra.

I believe the American people have found their edges with the rise of obesity, chronic disease, mental illness, and the lies of large corporations and politicians. We are now finding our center. We are starting to realize that our impact on Mother Earth impacts our well-being.

Good quality food starts with great soil, and great soil comes from organic and regenerative farming practices. There are so many conscious companies creating great products by investing in regenerative or organic farms, also valuing the people who work at these farms, ranches, and companies. I enjoy finding these companies and sharing them with my clients and friends. More and more people are starting to realize that we can save our planet by investing in our health. We can vote with our dollars and invest in our health. Because if we don't pay for our health now, we'll pay for our health later through sickness and disease (dis-ease).

My Dream

I dream that the holistic trainer will be the only kind of trainer. Being able to use breath-work to release trauma so that clients begin to create lasting change. Using energy works to further the healing process. Then after they cleared the body and mind of blocks, they would help the client integrate the messages they received through their healing process. The holistic trainer would be well versed in the concept of *'working in,'* which was made popular by Paul Chek.

Working in is when we use movement and breath to create more life force or chi to create balance in the body, the client would have an energy surplus. Qigong and Tai chi are forms of working in. Working out is when we use up that energy to build the body up, it will end in an energy deficit. Both are needed and utilized accordingly by eating nutrient-dense quality food over just counting calories and macros. The trainer would know that food is information for the body and that organic vegetables and fruits, pasture-raised meats, and wild-caught fish will have a different effect than their conventional counterparts. Quality water matters with the minerals we need. Bottled water or water from the tap causes hormonal imbalance. The trainer will teach the client about filtration and mineralization. Sleep isn't just about the hours we sleep, but the sleep quality. The trainer will teach proper sleep hygiene, knowing that sleep regulates hormones, recovery, and mental health. And finally, the trainer would have tools to teach clients how to change their negative thought patterns that are causing more distress in their lives. The holistic trainer should be the first person a person sees when they have health issues.

Now there is a big need for a holistic trainer. The current state of the world has brought awareness to the flaws of mainstream health and medical practices. I have witnessed firsthand that my approach has helped many people take control of their lives and heal from sickness of the mind, body, and spirit. And now I'm guiding more trainers and healers to do the same. It all starts with working on ourselves to become more conscious of our thoughts and actions. The holistic trainer will practice what they teach and will have their special gifts to share. Each has our unique spin on holistic coaching, but knowing the fundamentals: quality food, water, breathing, movement (working in and working out), quality sleep, and quality thoughts. I see the future as ancestral wisdom working alongside technology to create harmony in people's lives. We just had to find our edge to find our center.

~

SAYING:

"Anyone who is steady in his determination for the advanced stage of spiritual realization and can equally tolerate the onslaughts of distress and happiness is certainly a person eligible for liberation."

— A.C. Bhaktivedanta Swami Prabhupada,
The Bhagavad-Gita

MICHAEL BARRIOS

ABOUT THE AUTHOR

Michael Barrios is a Holistic Lifestyle Coach, Personal trainer, Somatic Release Breathwork Practitioner, and Energy Healer specializing in rapid, permanent change through corrective exercise, metabolic nutrition, breath-work, mindfulness practices, and energetic alignment. Using his heart-centered approach, he helps people feel strong, confident, and calm in their bodies for life-changing results. Through personal experience with many of the common struggles in a relationship, depression, trauma, and loss, Michael has risen and found his purpose in guiding others through their journey to finding their inner power and strength. Michael runs a Holistic gym, Morph-Fintness, in San Mateo, California, where he teaches trainers his approach and holds transformational breath-work classes, and visit him at Instagram:@miketheholsiticpa. Michael is a father, a healer, an intuitive, a researcher of esoteric practices, a partner, a student, a teacher, a lover, a poet, an athlete, a Filipino, a friend, and so much more.

You can contact him through email:
barrioscoaching@gmail.com

8

STARSEED SOUND HEALING

BY: MISTY PENNINGTON

"Looking Up. Kindness. Compassion. Beauty."

To me, being identified as a Starseed means being of qualities that linger in the light. The lightness of being -- Of having a lighter quality -- Moving upwards.

It's easy to get stuck in the past and what has happened and to try to prevent it from happening in our life again. However, something happens when we shift our focus forward, upward, onward.

Not in an attempt to design a perfect world - but looking towards openness, towards a field of possibility. Where things are not yet created but within the field of perspective possibilities.

.

.

I am a Starseed

Being a Starseed can mean a million things. For me, it's meant to embody the feminine aspects of myself to balance my energy. To bring the lightness of being to my being-ness. To be at one with the essence of who I am inherent, at my core - not what anyone else thinks I should be.

Sound healing has been instrumental for me in that work. The sacred instruments I use to create soundscapes, and all music in general, have been calling my awareness towards this field of possibility that I mentioned above.

The field of possibility holds the energy of CREATION. Sound healing, combined with extensive time in nature and my garden, has activated every cell in my body with creative juice.

"I believe the secret of embodying kindness, compassion, and beauty is achieved by attuning energetically to the frequency of creation."

When I am focused on creating, I'm peaceful. Inspired. Loving. Hopeful. Breathing deeply. Present in the moment at hand. Settled. Content. Curious. Gentle. Harmonious. Trusting. Grateful. Satiated. Passionate. Open-minded balanced with open-heartedness.

The longer moments that I settle into the energy of creation, the more deeply these feelings become embedded into my being. The less frustration, aggravation, and confusion I feel with myself and others.

I am more accepting.

This is the space where the divine feminine quality becomes my awareness. I switch to receiving mode. Instead of giving and doing, I am waiting and listening.

I believe I am creating a more loving and harmonious world by bringing awareness to the moment at hand in a receptive and creative space of feeling rather than from a space of fear and guilt. Fear and guilt usually mean I think about the past instead of the present.

I would say that my "societal programming" were built on paradigms of being fearful.

Stepping back, breathing deeply, softening my gaze, and transforming my intention to wait, and then listen, leads to observe more what comes up around me.

Worries or thoughts of things being something they weren't started to fall away as I engaged with what was currently happening.

Don't get me wrong, this led to some real serious transformation that required integrating learning to receive more intense emotions when I was not totally engaged.

I was willing to 'receive' and experience frequencies that didn't feel well or aligned with my well-being. This was my way of walking through that, and I found the energetic patterns in those situations and honed in on them. Then I allowed myself to feel when something didn't feel right or leaned into a 'this isn't the right feeling.'

Deep breathing is required at this point. I go to my breath when I feel guilt, fear, shame, or anger. I use energy medicine techniques to remind my body that I am safe enough to feel these feelings. Lengthening and deepening my breath brings a sense of calmness to my nervous system.

Then, I can lean into the feeling and find its source. This inquiry almost always reunites me with a version of my younger self that couldn't stick up for me when I felt ignored, betrayed, forgotten, or overlooked.

Then, I call upon today's knowledge and see how far I have

come. And I mentally hug that part of my younger self. I forgive myself for not knowing what I didn't know, and I share the wisdom of today and shift my thoughts, breathing into the field of possibility. I'm 'holding my own hand' while comforting the part of myself that was feeling off and aligning with the frequencies of possibility and creation. Bringing that part of myself forward and understanding that many more possibilities of outcome are available if I can open my heart to sensing them.

Dreaming Into the Field of Possibilities

I use this awareness, intermingled with the soft and soothing tones of sacred sound tools, to dream into the field of possibilities.

Doing this has created an openness in my world that didn't exist before. It hasn't been an easy path to walk, yet it's been one of the most fulfilling and rewarding for me. I'm learning to accept myself through depths of self-analysis that can feel endless.

I built the steps one at a time. Acknowledging bigger fears and bringing them to the doorstep of my awareness one at a time. Engaging in waiting and listening to feel, hear, and see what that fear was.

Allowing myself to feel uncomfortable feelings and inviting them into the realm of possibility somehow opened a window of understanding that if a tremendous fear could be a possible reality, couldn't the opposite, a miraculous joy, be a possible reality, too?

I can't force either reality - but how many possible realities are there?

As often as we make the smallest choices, another possible reality opens our perspective. If we were too busy worrying about the past or trying to create something for the future, I realized I might have missed what was available to me by focusing elsewhere.

Making a habit of slowing down and leaning into the current moment, especially as I began clearing away heavy thought patterns, emotions and behaviors, left me with nowhere else to focus but the current moment and the current choice.

Think about that! How incredible is that?

I immediately understood that I didn't want to let fear control which perspective I was looking for to create my next moment of reality. I wanted my inquiry about the possibility of joy to inspire the next choice I make.

Sacred Sounds of Crystal Singing Bowls

Listening to crystal singing bowls regularly helped me make this behavior an everyday practice as I became aware that I wanted to fine-tune my frequency, the sacred sound of the crystal bowls helped me relax into possibility.

The soothing sounds immediately helped calm my central nervous system. The beautiful harmonies soothed my mind, letting me drop deeper into my breath. If we're limiting our breath, we are holding on to tension in our physical body. Breathing more deeply has brought such rest to my physical body.

I became aware that if I wanted to make these changes permanent, I needed to SLOW WAY DOWN to tune into the subtlety of these frequencies.

It's so natural to be over-stimulated in our way of living that we often don't even know that we feel tense and nervous because we are conditioned to feel that way from a very young age. It's 'just how it seems to be.' It seems normal. Until we understand it isn't.

It takes a strong intention and a determined practice in our busy world to bring slowness to our lives. We are conditioned to live a fast-paced lifestyle. We have many opportunities to engage in slowing down and looking inward. Traveling more easily has allowed us to 'spread out' how we live.

Once we realize that we can still live a full, content life without running excessively, we can choose to change it. And there again, in this choice, a whole new field of possibility opens up before us.

Our super computer brain is quickly processing millions of bits of information in short periods. And when we choose something new, it requires an adjustment in our physical being to integrate that new frame of reference for ourselves. We do a lot of this on auto-pilot, and it becomes a habit.

Slowing down has made me more aware of the choices I am making on auto-pilot, and realizing that I want to be more aware and engaged with more of my choices.

Getting quiet, focusing my attention on a few moments of deep breathing, listening to soothing tones, consciously setting an intention to the field of possibilities, and breathing into it have changed my life dramatically for the better.

Sacred Sound Healing

The practice of 'sound frequency' is medicine, in my humble

opinion. *"Music and sound are keys to immediately influencing a frequency. All sound is frequency. And frequency is a key that unlocks a door of possibility."*

Sound Healing is using sound to purposely create frequencies that induce a state of awareness conducive to healing. Sound becomes sacred when we combine it with our prayerful intention.

I believe a person's frequency is determined by the alignment of their mind/body/soul. If my thoughts are inspired by emotions that feel light and loving, my behavior reflects that alignment. The same goes if my inspiration comes from heavy emotions. It's my personal experience that the frequency of sound interacts with my emotions, and my thoughts and physical body are also affected. Intention and focus on all three components of being in alignment is a powerful way of creating the life we wish to live.

Ethereal Magical Sound

A sound immersion can feel quite magical or ethereal.

I take my sound healing to another level by incorporating Reiki, toning, and other energy medicine techniques such as tapping or Donna Eden Medicine protocols. These tools work beautifully together, creating a harmonious environment for your mind, body, and spirit to resonate easily into that field of possibility.

It is very easy to get caught up in the drama of events that are going on as our world is changing. We are facing many challenges as we transform outdated systems that need reconfiguring. As we move forward into the future, I believe purposely tuning into frequencies that feel uplifting is necessary for our well-being. Doing that from a place of love and possibility will directly impact the smoothness of transformation we experience.

Come and join me in using your voice, intention, and energy to create a higher vibration in the collective energies.

MISTY PENNINGTON

ABOUT THE AUTHOR

Misty Pennington is a Sound Alchemist, Master and Certified Usui/Holy Fire Reiki, and Karuna Reiki. Her modalities create transformative private or group sessions. She opened her healing space in St Peters, MO, in 2017.

She traveled around Missouri as a guest to yoga studios and meditation centers, sharing her Reiki and Sound vibration modality through Crystal Tones-Singing Bowls as a guide that supports her clients through harmonizing soundscapes into deep states of relaxation. As a compassionate healer, she successfully navigate the winding path of learning to love themselves unconditionally. It also helped her achieve a deep state of mental and physical well-being (moving out of anxiety) by focusing on her creative life while passionate about gardening and rituals that intersect celebrations on natural living.

Misty holds a Bachelor of Arts Degree in Human Resources, a lifelong student of the mystery of life, creating a safe space that helps her clients discover patterns that contribute to connection, harmony, and satisfaction in their ways of being. Before all this, Misty was a financial secretary at a public school district in 2015 and retired from a 32-year career.

Misty@Gardenofcommonground.com

9

THE PURSUIT AND ENJOYMENT OF HAPPINESS

BY: BYRON BRADLEY CARRIER

I wanted to punch Shri Rajneesh (later to be called Osho) in the nose, pull back my fist, and ask him a question: *"If we are not the body, it and the world all being the illusion of maya, would you mind if I punch you in the nose again?"*

I didn't, of course. I had nothing against him personally; mine was a philosophical dispute. He gave a small group of us darshan in a small hotel room in Bombay (now Mumbai), India, in the summer of 1972. He wore impeccable whites. He had calm, beautiful eyes. Many adoring women sat at his feet. He sported a huge diamond watch. He went on about maya being unimportant, yet he did so from his supportive world of sumptuous beauties and fantastic wealth.

I was sick of being sick. I had lost 25 pounds in India. I hadn't avoided their food. I dressed in common Indian garb. On my own, I had gone from Gujrat to Delhi and back, finding out how *'full of it'* I was. I had seen the clean poorness of the villages and the filthy poverty of the cities. Flies everywhere. Rivers ferment from all the waste in them. Beggar children pointing their stub arms at me with a pleading look. It was a land of saints and flies, peacocks and vultures.

I had gone to India disgusted with western religion. Its historic role was to intercede between the peasants and the king, protecting his power and wealth while promising *'pie in the sky'* for the overworked peasants. I was enamored with eastern religion and Jungian psychology, hoping they made religion pertinent to this precious home of a planet.

I had gone to India with my guru friend, Dr. Vasavada, a Jungian therapist new to the University of Chicago area, where I was in seminary. His guru, the Blind Saint of Vrindavan, had received me graciously. He didn't mind my rude question: *"What's it like to be a saint? How is it different for any of us?"* His interpreters balked. He laughed, *"A saint is a member of the universal human family."*

Robbed at his ashram, I sold my remaining luggage to a luggage seller and took the 3rd class Midnight Express train from Delhi back to Bombay. Housed with a Vasavada family member in a posh apartment overlooking the Parsi Towers of Silence (where dead bodies are left for the birds) I stumbled into that Rajneesh darshan. He was notorious in India, but a few dozen Americans and Europeans sat in awe. Outside, about a mere mile away, a thousand souls tried to live in their tin and cardboard huts. One water spicket for everybody. No toilet.

So, I reacted to his smug, privileged stance. My sickened body, those bodies of the truly poor, that beautiful but polluted land – all these welled up in me, making me want to punch him. It seemed to me the West got duped into pining for the afterlife, while the East went for the instead-of-life. Why love the body or the land if they're just a stepping stone or an illusion? The goal of life is to become the atman, the Self we are within the many bodies we allegedly reincarnate into.

I didn't punch him, and over time I came to respect his daring teachings. Before leaving that darshan, his followers invited me to their dawn meditation on the beach. Sick, I couldn't imagine getting up early to sit on a cold beach. That morning I had a dream of people dancing wildly around a big fire at a beach. Years later, I learned that's the sort of meditation they did.

My return to the United States was more of a culture shock than India had been. Fat, frantic people scurried from one indulgence to another, never satisfied. The waste of resources pursuing a desperately empty life offended my frugal sense.

The eldest of five siblings, I grew up in Michigan using as few sheets of toilet paper as possible. Use minimal resources; don't waste. Pontiac was an abandoned industrial town in the suburbs of Detroit. The *"pure and sparkling stream"* that Alexis de Tocqueville admired had become an oily river strewn with tires and rotten car parts. Oakland Lake had gone from muskrats, big bass, and gar pike to a barren, weed-choked swamp with only the remnants of life present. Yet, there I discovered that burying food scraps in the yard promoted worms and better soil. I replenished a bit of soil with scraps that would have been wasted.

I had been warned by 1984, Brave New World, and All Quiet on the Western Front. I had been inspired by E. F. Schumacher's Small is Beautiful. 'Mother Earth News' showed how sustainably we could live. Psychedelics opened me to the cosmic beauty and profound meaning of simple sand, flowers, and sunshine. Beatniks, hippies, and back-to-the-landers were reconnecting to their bodies and our lands. An affluent life wasn't as important as a fulfilled, ethical, happy one.

Back in India, I remembered how interested Indians were in the hordes of affluent long hair westerners coming from America and Europe, modern versions of Gautama, the Buddha. The wandering hippies in India seemed to reincarnate his story. He also eschewed a life of privileged ease to pursue spiritual truth and alignment. He didn't suppose God or impose his authority. He merely beckoned others to an ethical and fulfilled life. Pursuing and fulfilling desires won't get it.

Gandhi had said life will satisfy our need but not our greed. What does it take to have a healthy, happy life? Material wealth doesn't guarantee spiritual success. But who is pursuing which? A poor farmer of an Indian village can get more from his or her breathing than a billionaire does.

The engines of an industrialized consumer economy will pump out cheap stuff made to soon break and be replaced. At what cost to our ecosystem? The materials, energy, and labor used go to what purpose? Do a few rich warrant the ecological and social cost? If we move the carbon created by ancient sunlight over millions of years from below the ground into our sky in a mere century, thereby creating climate disasters, would a booming economy justify the lasting harm? How dare we stress the future for a meager present?

We're slow to realize the enormity of time and space science now explains. It was a cozy world, God in the clouds, hell below, all of it spinning around us, the center of the universe. We are that, but only if you realize *any* center seems *the* center in an infinite universe. Historian of religions Mircea Eliade noted the pole at the center of the village marked the center of the world. However, all poles in all villages also did that. We each and all come from a sense of center, an "*I*" with a name and story encountering an endless array of other "*I*'s, each with their own view. A lifetime of that view seems like a lot, but in the evolutionary and geologic time scale, we've brief lives on a planet that is pretty small.

Yet, how reliably our planet spins as it travels around our bounteous sun, perfectly balanced to rouse up resplendent, magnificent, interrelated life. Our lives, *"three-score and ten, or by reason of strength, fourscore,"* are an ample stay on a planet that will reliably spin just like it does. But how? Extracting and exhausting limited resources in a frantic orgy of numb effort? Planting a garden that all will enjoy? What does it really take to have a good life?

Bhutan attempts to ask and answer this. Instead of a Gross Domestic Product, they extensively measure the four pillars of Gross National Happiness: fair and sustainable socio-economic development; conservation and promotion of a vibrant culture; environmental protection; and good governance. Being very poor, they don't rank very high in the UN's assessment of which countries promote the most happiness. Finland and Denmark get the highest scores; Afghanistan is near the lowest. Bhutan is hard to measure, and some measures put it at 79th. But that it pursues happiness, measuring and adjusting as it goes signals a whole new standard on the good life.

Instead of plugging away in a competitive society strewn with scarcity and stress, what if we loved each other and our planet so much that everything we did served the common good? What if we were to do as God suggests in the opening Bible chapter, *"Replenish the Earth?"* Sustainability is a popular word. What if we took it further? Instead of barely keeping even what if we were to replenish so skillfully and abundantly we built automatic abundance into the why and how of our lives? How rich could our soils get? How healthy are the oceans? How many fish in the rivers? How diverse and abundant are the animals? How well-off, healthy, and happy are the people?

When Europeans discovered the New World, it seemed a bounteous paradise of limitless resources: endless trees, animals, and fish. But even the infinite ocean and endless sky were in fact limited. Soils that took thousands of years to grow were plowed up and blown away. Bison skulls piled into mini mountains. Passenger pigeons were shot to extinction for the mere fun of it. Slaves spent lifetimes furthering someone else's fortune; today they're the poor, trying to get by in *'right to work'* states. How advanced are we if there are less fish in our streams and lakes than were here when we arrived?

"This is the dawning of the Age of Aquarius," we sang and felt.

Perhaps it is, only it's taking longer than we hoped. A resurgence of worldwide fascism glares from Brazil to Boston. Instead of exporting windmills and solar panels, we're exporting armaments. Some of our religions promote the vilest persons to the highest powers. Angry, armed people attack the temple of our democracy and crazed gunmen explode the bodies of babies with their protected weapons of war.

Fear, hate, and self-righteous reactionary opinion seem to have invaded our midbrains, amygdales afire. Rage is all the rage. But it isn't new. Jesus dealt with the Romans. Freethinkers endured the Inquisition. Women eluded the witch hunts. Julian Assange is guilty until proven innocent, punished for decades without a trial. Journalists write the truth and get assassinated. Such fears cloud and misdirect our vision.

Another view sees a corner being turned, an era being ended, a new time being born. Psychology used to dwell on pathology. Now, positive psychology metes out the tools of happier lives. *'Drugs'* were an excuse to oppress and jail whole populations. Now, psychedelic therapies make use of ancient entheogens to radically end depression and addiction. THC, MDMA, LSD, 5 MeO DMT, Ibogaine, Ketamine and more are not problem substances to be suppressed, they're sacraments of the soul. Technologically, we can now drive on sunlight, wasting nothing, polluting nothing. Ecologically, we are learning how to replenish the soil, replant diverse forests, and restock the oceans. We exploited and injured Eden, but Eden is resilient. When loved, it bounces back with beauteous abundance.

Our souls are not some ghosts that float away when we die. Soul meant movement, blood pumped, synapses aligned, breath easy and glad. Our souls are enmeshed in life. Those around us, the food we eat, the ideas we think with – all these serve or starve our soul. The technologies we use, the governments we create, the arts we generate, the causes that we partake – all these fulfill or frustrate our soul. The inside reflects the outside, and it is from the inside that we steer the outside.

"We all pursue happiness."

We all pursue happiness. Buddha taught '*pursuing* it isn't *enjoying*' it. Pursuing it by running rough-shod over others, wasting resources for frivolous purposes, seeking pleasure when it isn't right – all these dull our souls. Enjoying our breath, seeing soul in others, honoring the nature that births and sustains us – these bring out souls alive. After all, it's our birthright, we are, as our Founders affirmed, *"Endowed by our Creator life, liberty and pursuit of happiness."*

I didn't want to hurt Rajneesh. Only later, in Netflix's "Wild, Wild Country" did I learn of his epic story. My reaction was against the way eastern and western religions fail to help us live up to our once-in-a-lifetime incarnation. The center is the same in all, yet each center is unique, a body, a story, a calling. The good Lord wants us all happy. We're learning how to live up to that in ways that promote the happiness of all, that loves Eden back, and brings our precious incarnation to its fuller enjoyment.

~

BYRON BRADLEY CARRIER

ABOUT THE AUTHOR

Byron Bradley Carrier was born in Pontiac, Michigan on the day Hiroshima was bombed in Japan. That horrid event formed a background theme for him, a warning on how wrong we humans can get. He migrated from art to funeral directing, fifty years as a liberal Unitarian Universalist minister. Now he is retired from that and speaks and writes in his own voice. What is important for us humans at this point in history to address?

His passion is to help us relate well to ourselves, those around us, our given society, and our one and only environment. He is honored to participate for the third time in the Awakening Starseeds series.

You can read his bio, peruse his writings, and contact him at his website: https://www.earthlyreligion.com/about-the-founder/

10

HEALING MOVEMENT

BY: MICHELLE WOODRUFF

Seiki Tapping

I never fit inside the box. Even when I was training in classical dance 8 hours a day with evening and weekend rehearsals, I didn't belong. I struggled with choreography. It always felt forced and unnatural for me. I was drawn to movement but didn't know why. My focus was not solely on performance, and at the time, my focus on movement evaded me. Yet, I was intrinsically drawn to dance, move, and express. However, it was about teaching that experience to others that ignited the fire within me, teaching others how to overcome the limitations of their bodies and movement patterns. Those techniques that most interested me were not ballet, tap, jazz, and modern dance, but the somatic approaches. I connected with Feldenkrais, Pilates, and Alexander techniques-all with huge somatic aspects.

It wasn't until the summer of 1998 that I realized there was another form of dance expression. A form with no rules or technical approaches. I was a physical therapist assistant and attended a week-long Myofascial Release Seminar by John F. Barnes, PT. It was located at Lake of the Ozarks, in Missouri. I am drawn to nature, and the lake was the perfect setting for discovering my *"True connection"* to movement. On the second day of the seminar, we practiced a particular myofascial technique. We had been paired up for a practice/learning break-out session. It was generally quiet during the break-out sessions, with John verbally guiding us through applying the myofascial techniques. My body intensely propelled into a dance with no warning or indication whatsoever. Not a dance led by my mind, but by my spirit. My body began to spontaneously move in a manner that appeared to be ritualistic.

My movement was well-grounded, with intense positioning, seemingly impossible positions, and almost acrobatic in nature. It was a strong and forceful movement that cleared the entire space of the room. Others stopped their break-out session to yield to what was occurring. I quickly broke contact with my practice partner and, with eyes closed, was thrashing about in a primitive, indigenous manner. I was praising the ground while contorting and executing unpredictable direction changes. I was fully engaged in this movement, riding the energy wave. It came from inside me. It was uninhibited. It felt exhilarating. John himself had to approach me energetically to calm and contain the energy pulsing through the movements. I remember him asking my practice partner how she felt about what had happened, and she replied, "I was mad because I lost control." Therein was her lesson. It was my first experience with Seiki. Many may call it *"Trance dance,"* but I now know that it was Seiki. The energy emanated from inside me and aligned my system for optimal health. I felt renewed, exhilarated, and blissful. The following week, I became pregnant with my daughter. I often wonder if the energy alignment from that Seiki experience contributed to the ease of my conception.

My entire life prepared me for this particular moment in time. While in elementary school, I saw a detective television program where the villain was a dancer. This episode aired during Halloween week. The villain wore a cape and was touted as a vampire because he was capable of leaping from one building top to another. Upon the conclusion of the episode, the villain, in reality, was a dancer.

I asked my mother, *"Why was he able to leap from one building to another?"* She replied, *"Because he is a dancer, dancers can leap great distances."* I became fascinated with the body's ability to execute extraordinary feats from that moment. It was then that I decided I wanted to train to dance.

I lived in a small town with no dance studio. I relentlessly asked my mother to take dance lessons. That opportunity did not arise until I was in junior high school (7th grade). Finally, after years of waiting, a small dance studio opened in my hometown. I was enrolled and started to learn ballet, tap, and jazz dance. I loved the idea that I could make my body move rhythmically, unlike most people I knew. I participated in speech and drama during my high school years and enjoyed competing in improvisational competitions. I was cast in several plays and musicals and became a choreographer for the school musicals. I fell in love with expression through movement. In my senior year of high school, I was accepted into the dance and theater program at Webster University in St. Louis, MO.

Although I was interested in dance, science was greatly important to me. The biological sciences piqued my curiosity. I would study for a test 3 days in advance. I had a photographic memory and could remember the notes I took in class. When it was time for an exam, I could visually recall the page of my notes with the subject matter and read the answer from the pages in my mind. I took all the advanced biological courses I could: biology I and II, zoology, botany, and human physiology (my ultimate favorite). Biologies were not only stimulating for me but easy to remember. I can still, to this day, recall the formula for cellular respiration, and it has been 40 years. Maybe I can relate to cellular respiration because of the release of energy.

Energy is everything and releasing energy from the inside through movement was *"My thing."* I can't say that the energy wave follows any particular rules other than utilizing movement to align and heal the body. Indigenous peoples around the globe have used similar forms of dance or movement to address healing and spirituality in unison. Dance is more than an artistic expression, it is a spiritual expression, and it doesn't have to follow any rules. When did humanity move away from this form of expression, something inherent in ancient cultures?

The practice and application of Reiki have been used for centuries. Where does Seiki differ from Reiki? Reiki is a subtle energy approach. Seiki is far from subtle. In the book Seiki Jutsu, The Practice of Non-Subtle Energy Medicine by Bradford and Hillary Keeney (2014), Bradford Keeney, following the tradition of Ikuko Osumi Sensei, describes his lifelong relationship with Seiki. He discusses how he opens himself to the Seiki energy and allows it to present and move his non-subtle body. Seiki energy can present itself in chanting, yelling, moving, clapping, or any bold expression of the individual. That expression is unique to the individual in that it is what that person needs for the Seiki healing energy to rise and move through the body. So many times in society, we restrain ourselves. We hold back our exuberant expressions of joy or happiness because of the unwritten social rules that such expression is unacceptable. But why is it not acceptable? I find it not only acceptable but contagious. Seiki moves through one person and can easily jump to another simultaneously. It offers a unique experience that can elevate each person if allowed to spread. My approach is to open individuals to the Seiki experience, to teach them how to allow the Seiki to rise throughout their body and transform their energy from the inside out, all while yelling, clapping, stomping, singing, and dancing. Seiki is fun, and the experience is freeing. It fills the energetic and healing needs of the participant.

For me, Seiki evolved. As I opened myself to the Seiki experience, more components presented themselves. The final component that I added to the Seiki experience was that of Tapping. While taking an EFT/Tapping seminar sponsored by Dawson Church's EFT Universe organization, I found another natural, somatic approach that resonated within my soul. The BA that I received from Webster University in 1987 was a dual degree. Webster University was one of the few, and maybe the only University at the time to offer dual degrees. I received my BA in both dance and counseling psychology. At the time, I wanted to work in the field of dance therapy. When I graduated from Webster in 1987, dance therapy was in its infancy with no direct path to certification. It was not widely recognized, though I had familiarized myself with every ounce of published research and application. It seemed a natural connection between mind, body, spirit, and dance therapy had significant rehabilitative benefits. As there was a lack of a clear-cut program to become a dance therapist, I taught classical dance for a short time at Culver Stockton College in northeast Missouri. One of the most exciting experiences I had was a collaborative modern dance work with a kinetic sculpture created by Sculptor Grant Kenner (1919-2001). The commute was 2 hours in each direction, and it was a difficult situation to continue. Shortly after that, I began teaching classical dance in Chesterfield, MO, at Krupinski Academy of Dance. I remained there until my next call from spirit. Still embodying a keen interest in a somatic approach to movement, I returned to college and received an AAS as a physical therapist assistant. I used Alexander Technique daily to instruct movement patterns to my patients effectively.

Most recently, my approach to healing evolved into what I now call Seiki Tapping. Seiki Tapping is a culmination of my life experiences in movement and healing. I begin each session with EFT/Tapping to remove any limiting beliefs or energetic barriers to the Seiki process itself. It improves the participant's comfort level with the self-expression inherent in the Seiki Tapping sessions. Following the Tapping, I present the 8 Principles of Mystic Dance given to me through meditation. Each movement clears and opens a specific chakra/energy center in the body. It also improves the participants' comfort level with bold vocalizations as self-expression through Seiki. The Principles align the chakras, allowing the Seiki to easily move inside the participant's body. Each chakra has a verbal phrase and movement when executing the 8 Principles. We repeat the Principles movement pattern with accompanying vocalizations for three cycles.

The vocalizations correspond to the following chakras:
NAH TAY- Crown Chakra
KUN DA LAY- Third Eye Chakra
EH MET- Throat Chakra
SHAH TAY- Heart Chakra
ET- Solar Plexus Chakra
MA TAH- Pelvic Chakra
SHE SAY- Associated with the Right Side Root Chakra
MAY TAY- Associated with the Left Side Root Chakra

When I connected with the higher realms during meditation for more information regarding the 8 Principles of Mystic Dance, I questioned why there were 8 Principles and why the Root Chakra was divided into a left and right. The response I received was, *"It is known in the higher realms that there are 8 Chakras of the Human Energy System, with the 8th being the most esoteric."* The Root Chakra is addressed in both right and left approaches as it is the balance of the masculine and the feminine that is necessary at this time. Be it known that One will notice that the movement pattern associated with the right Root Chakra is presented in a counterclockwise direction. In contrast, the movement associated with the left Root Chakra is presented clockwise. The union of these two forms a figure 8 pattern that affects the Torus structure of energy surrounding the individual. It may be so that an individual may experience a reversal in these directions based on the specific energy pattern of the individual. The energy would then present clockwise on the right Root Chakra and counterclockwise on the left Root Chakra. One is to determine which direction best suits them and use that approach. As the energy travels in figure 8 patterns with the application of Reiki, so does this pattern present itself in the rise of the Seiki. "THAT IS ALL."

Participants assume the access position following the 8 Principles of Mystic Dance execution. My guru Shri Mataji Nirmala gave me this position while in meditation. The position is similar to the position utilized by Bradford Keeney but with a slight variation. The access position involves positioning both hands to be held in a specific manner while contacting each side of the nose bridge, with one thumb on each side. The third, fourth, and fifth fingers are interlocked while the index fingers and thumbs are extended. The index fingers and thumbs contact the opposing side at the fingertips. It is then that the thumbs are placed to contact on each side of the nose bridge, between the nose and the eye. The head is then slightly bowed.

The final step is to allow the Seiki to move through your body and follow the Seiki's movement pattern or wave with music accompanying or not. It can involve movement, vocalization, shaking, clapping, and yelling. Any non-subtle movement or expression is possible. I generally like to use indigenous music to raise the Seiki, although I have also used rock music. It depends on what I am seeing in the participant(s). Seiki is allowed to move, and eventually, the intention is set to slow down and finally halt the Seiki movement. The feeling afterward is often indescribable. Many describe it as *'Feeling lighter'* or *'more grounded.'* I have yet to understand how one experience can result in opposing feelings.

The experience is different for each person. As the Seiki is allowed to rise through the body, it aligns the energy system, clears the chakras, and stimulates healing. It rises like a wave from the base of the spine as it moves through the participant. The participant does not direct it but allows it. I kept the Seiki tucked inside myself for many years, not realizing my life was about freeing that energy and movement. I would adhere to the rules of others, only to find it unnatural for my expression. I do not underestimate the practice of structured dance or movement but instead, allow others to experience what they may need for their true expression and healing. Seiki Tapping will bring a participant's life and energy blockages to the forefront. What presents itself in a Seiki Tapping session reflects what is needed to move forward in life. I tell my clients, *"What holds you back in Seiki Tapping is what holds you back in life."*

As new Cosmic and Earth energies move through us, they allow us to clap, yell, shout, jump, vibrate, wiggle, and whatever else is called upon. When did our culture stop expressing this healing energy? I now understand my intense attraction to indigenous dancing. These cultures held the key to healing, and there are still many indigenous healers today in our world. It is time to recognize them and recognize the Seiki, for there is great power in the Seiki energy.

SAYING:

"A gift is pure when it is given from the heart to the right person at the right time and at the right place, and when we expect nothing in return"

—The Bhagavad Gita

MICHELLE WOODRUFF

ABOUT THE AUTHOR

Michelle Woodruff, Energy Healer and Practitioner, Podcaster, Author

With 30 years in traditional healthcare, Michelle Woodruff has a history of bridging traditional and complementary medicine. She fused traditional and complementary medicine to assist clients in healing through body, mind, emotion, and spirit. Her background in the holistic rehabilitative aspects of orthopedics and neurology successfully allowed her to work with patients through the full life spectrum. She received the AMTA Missouri Chapter Meritorious Award for her work with public agencies.

Michelle instructed therapists, patients, physicians, teachers, parents, caregivers, and nurses, by providing a unique insight into healing and its relationship to the human energy system. Her intuitive abilities provide a unique approach to healing. She presented her skills at the Born to Learn National Conference for Parents as Teachers and the Missouri Chapter for the Association of Developmental Disabilities.

A lifelong medium, Michelle has been able to connect with higher realms since childhood. She has communicated with Spirit Guides, Akashic Masters, and Angels for much of her life -- providing Energy Health Readings, Integrative Bodywork Sessions, EFT/Tapping, and Seiki Tapping. She is also the author of the multicultural, inclusive children's book The Magical Gift From Santa, which instills the gift of giving in children. Her podcast, Trucking Through Life, provides guidance and education for those beginning to open to their higher gifts. You can learn more about Michelle on her website.

magicmichellewoodruff.com.

11

MAYAN GALACTIC TIMEKEEPER

BY: JOSE FEDERICO AJPU MUÑOZ

"A Time Traveler's Journey of 66,000 Years."

When I Left Atl'Antix on the day of 4 Ajpu, it was the end of the cycle and the beginning of the Future. The elders in the Council of the 13 Tribes gather all 33,000 of us at the Ship Port for final instructions to survive what is coming and establish the world's new Tulan across the oceans in all directions.

THE INSTRUCTIONS

Tribe 13, Tribe 12, and Tribe 11 will go to the Above (the galaxies). Tribes 10 and 9 will go to Middle Earth and build Xibalba (sheebaelbae). Tribes 8 and 7 will go to the Purple Mountains in the West (North Central and South America). Tribes 6 and 5 will go to the East across the more dangerous waters to the Caxcaxian Snowy Mountains, and Tribes 4 and 3 will go to the unknown territories of the North.

Finally, with a grim concern on his face, Elder Ik Ak'ab'al (Night Winds) assigned his three daughters, Jade Princess, Purple Flower, and Tzochitl. Pilat'zi Kat'zin to the territories of the cold South.

We were expecting fire-rain from the heavens that starry night to anticipate the final trumpet announcement. Fire Butterfly and Rainbow Butterfly insisted we had time to go up the creek to play Xillion, our favorite game.

As usual, Fire Butterfly had an excellent reason why we should follow her since. She was, in any case, the young commander of our ship going to the Purple Mountain out west. She made a good point—indeed, we did have to go around the river and into the ship by the Ocean, and indeed, we still had some time to spare.

Everything became eerily quiet when we were about to pull out our liquid light stones from our scarlet, blue, and rainbow pouches. We looked at each other, and before we could say anything, massive meteorites came down from above and out from below. Thrown apart from each other by tall earth waves produced by our Mother Earth-shaking, we lay on the ground once we realized it was helpless to try to remain standing.

That was the darkest night on this planet 66,222 cycles ago.

We Waited

We waited for the shaking to stop, but the strange noises Mother Earth kept producing kept throbbing between our ears. Across a newly made crack, Tzochitl was the first to get up and quickly started gathering brothers and sisters trying to get to higher ground.

We collected ourselves and surrounded Fire Butterfly for instructions. She calmly levitated and established telepathic communication with all tribes to assess the situation. Her soft blue eyes fixed down the valley leading to the port while the rest of us, in disbelief, supported our thoughts in the hope of getting a grip of the magnitude of the events.

Unusual strong winds blew right through her curly orange-red long hair. Fire Butterfly ascended to the ground and told us there was no time to go back to the ship leaving west, pointing her Red Staff towards the Ocean as Earth's most vigorous shaking began. Her thunderous voice summoned the 3 Sisters. In disbelief, we watched half of the entire valley break away from us, capsizing into the Ocean with everything that was on it.

She removed her rocket wings, handing them and her Red Staff to Purple Flower. Just as we handed the Liquid Knowledge Crystals to Tzochitl, Fire Butterfly asked Rainbow Butterfly and me to give up our winged rockets. She then asked Jade Princess to give her rocket wings (our individual Transportation device) to Maruxca, the newly appointed leader of the survivors. She said, "You have to get to the Purple Mountain, and from there use the stepping stones lands (now known as the Caribbean Islands) until you get to the land where you will establish Tulan, Tulan Tzu, Tulan Ri, and Tulan Qi."

In silence, Fire Butterfly, Jade Princess, Rainbow Butterfly, and I held our hands and watched as the 3,300 survivors descended in slow motion, led by Maruxca. As Purple Flower and Tzochitl took off into the air, the rest of the valley submissively succumbed into the Ocean. We were the only ones that remained.

Remember Who You Are And Why You Are Here

What really happened on December 21, 2012? Here we are in 2022 at the precipice of *"The End of All Endings And The Beginning Of All Beginnings."* We live in a great time of transformation as Humanity has become closer through technology, yet we are more distant than ever. Society has fallen out of rhythm with the Earth's natural cycles. People seek spiritual guidance as many of us have forgotten where we came from and where we are going. Where do we find the answers in these uncertain times?

"Our Butterflies-Memoirs Through Space and Time" is a portal that allows us to remember where we came from through a Mayan Day Keeper's visions and memories. We are allowed to enter intimate moments that seem familiar. It's that deja vu feeling - that I know I have lived this before. Where does destiny meet free will? Is one really given an assignment before birth?

These are questions that arise through the memoirs. When the Day Keeper must leave his only true love, Hummingbird, there is a clash between what was assigned and what was desired in the heart. However, time continues, and so does the curse of the day keeper.

There is a tragedy when the trajectory does not line up in time. However, a curse can be a blessing. The butterflies show us that time does not exist in a single plain as they bend through empty space. They remind us of the infinite potential we hold over our free will. Also, we are just as powerful as the cosmos and can change the course of our destiny. When we are open to remembering, we can see that eternal love is the password that allows us to enter these portals.

In the places of the greatest darkness, Hummingbird emerges to remind us that we are the light and that when you light the way for another, you also light the way for yourself. Perhaps Hummingbird knew she would see the Day Keeper again and again in the invisible abyss of eternal love.

The codecs revealed in the memoirs provide a way to measure the distant memories that only the ancient spirits recall. The Day Keeper reminds us that the illumination period began after turning the fires on the sacred day of Ajpu 4. The day is known as the end of the world, and "*December 21, 2012, would mark the beginning of the road towards a new era of 26,000 years - the beginning of a new world of radiant love, peace, and harmony.*"

The Ceremony For Eternity

We know, now is the moment to be grateful for all the ones who left to the unknown to build the New World, the Fourth World. Fire Butterfly spoke of how we had to honor the Elders' final request to have all survivors go through the 13 Gates while their vortexes were still open. She was the only one left who had the wisdom to execute such a task. First, we must make it to the Red Rivers Mountain.

However, without our winged rockets and not enough collective power to levitate all the survivors, we, the four messengers, will have to resort to primal techniques to survive the 5 long-run distances (One long run = 100 miles) and save as many of the survivors as possible.

We saw the heartbreaking decision fall on the shoulders of the young commander. There is no time to think about what's right or wrong. There is only time to do our job and push as many people as possible up the mountain.

The breaking apart of the land had now created a different

surface to walk on. Whereas one-time beautiful valleys lay, in a moment, the land transformed and crushed together in the shape of rippling, rolling new mountains. The once underground rivers instantly started flooding the few left flatlands, creating a small buffer against the mountain. Tall waves were rapidly approaching behind us.

Fire Butterfly and Jade Princess, the fastest runners, were in front of a long line of tired, hungry, but determined pack of survivors. Rainbow Butterfly and I were at the very last of the line, pushing the weakened children and elderly to go forward.

We arrived at the first Fire River to see it had gotten wider, the Emerald Green Bridge showing faintly as a tiny path through the steaming flowing lava from the Fire Mountain. More than half of the survivors are gone, mostly washed away to the sea and fallen into the abyss of newly created deep cracks as the ground split open. Again, we gather to get a sense of our new situation.

We gather everyone's supplies and enjoy our last sacred refreshing water and nutritious food. Barely able to stand due to the continuous shaking, we see five other people led by a familiar face, my brother's wife, the Love Butterfly. She is carrying the Blue Crystal Cranium and the news that my brother's ship has been able to leave safely. Her duty right now is to bring the last three Rain Children (rain-making wisdom keepers) to the 13 Gates (portals to other dimensions and universes from the Past and the Future). We are at this moment a remaining 44 survivors in what is left of the once-powerful and beautiful 33 long runs on the big island. We begin to cross the roaring river; however, not everyone makes it to the still-standing giant Ceiba trees (trees of life).

As we walk closer to the vortex, we hear increasing humming frequencies. We feel the rushing energy going through us from above and into Mother Earth. We see the giant trunks of the trees are now in the shape of softly twisting columns (whenever you see a tree's twisted trunk, there is a portal to go|beyond imagination). Brothers and sisters gather. We are here. The 20 pyramids are still standing, forming the most sacred space in the center. The survivors from the circle quickly in the middle of the sacred space.

The four of us—Rainbow Butterfly, Jade Princess, Love Butterfly, and I—stand forming a smaller square, giving the space to Fire Butterfly in the absolute middle. In a single motion, everyone puts their left knee down and hands up as we start the ceremony with our ancestors' prayer.

Our Ancestors' Prayer For Our Rebirth

"Sachaj la numaj Tioshie.
Sachaj la Numac Santo Mundo.
Quin ya'o ri numulla nurigalo.
Chiwach La Tioshies chiwach Santo Mundo.
Quinyo'owa jun nacera candelas.
Nu ta'cabal pari akan kab la Tioshies.
Kab La Tiosh La Tiosha
chire lebal k'ij
chaka jibal k'ij
cajyucut kaj
cajyucut ulew
Sa'j la rech c'ut nuchac nu patan"

"We know you forgive us, Creator and Creatress.
We know you forgive us, Sacred World.

We are giving you what we have; please
accept our prayers and offerings.
In your presence Creator and Creatress,
In your presence Sacred World.
Please accept these first fire crystals.
These are our offerings to you, Creator,
at the rising Sun, at the setting Sun, the corners of the sky, and
the corners of the Earth.
Come and accept our lives of service."

Now Rise, Brothers And Sisters!

We will leave this planet to come back and live 20 more times. Together, we will journey the road to eternal love and 20 more visits to this sacred world. When we leave the physical, we together chant DOR-E-LIL-LA for 6 round circles. Together, the 3 physical elements, the 3 astral elements, and the 3 mind elements.

Let's calm our minds; conscious of our freedom from the flesh, we think of the words LA-UM-I-L. "We now stand in front of the 13 gates of the immortals. Here we go together, and I, Fire Butterfly, will guide you through the Gate of Fire.

MEKUT-EL-SHAB-EL-HALE. SUR-BEN-EL-ZABRUT. ZIN-E FRIM-QUAR-EL.

"We are the light. In us, there is no darkness. We are free of the bondage of night. OPEN the 13 gates so we may pass to the wisdom realm. We are the light. For us, there are no barriers. We command OPEN. EDOM-EL-AHIM-SOBBERT-ZUR-ADOM." The ground opened, creating a circling mix of our offerings and light blue rays growing bigger and bigger. The 28 survivors, including the 3 rain children, went through the gate first. The swirling circle became small enough for the 5 of us to hold hands.

See You In The Ancient Future

We all must remember where we came from, where we are now and where we are going.

As contained in this Chapter, these sacred memories will assist anyone with an open heart, mind, and spirit in remembering how to see Past, Present, and Future simultaneously. They are a spiritual memory trigger and an open invitation to simultaneously see the Past, Present, and the Future, when we are open to receiving the messages behind the words to free ourselves from time and space-locked boundaries.

These codecs will help you establish in your mind, body, Soul, and spirit a clear memory of creation happening in the eternal present, cause and effect happening at the same time, and also destiny and free will are in the same space where we choose to create the best Future for ourselves, family, community and everything that exists.

I am certain that the many thousands of butterflies who choose to remember and come together recognize each other and deliver Mothership Earth to a state of balance, unity, joy, peace, and intergalactic harmony.

Using the Sacred Mayan Calendars To Reveal Who You Are

As we continue to decipher the coded instructions in the Mayan Croix, we align ourselves with universal true time, and we flow with the new frequencies arriving daily to our Mothership Earth stronger and faster than ever from distant galaxies and dimensions. Within this Croix codex, any individual can find a navigational map to better oneself and be of the highest service to Humanity.

In the sacred Calendar, we have the opportunity to see ourselves in the Past, Present, and Future in a multidimensional way at the same time. There are three timelines: Past, Present, and Future; 15 dimensions as we each have at least 15 virtues to discover, 5 in each timeline.

When we choose to use this sacred Calendar, we honor our Past, Present, and Future and honor those around us. When we practice these ways, we are honoring the space-time directions, we honor all elements, all forces of nature, and we honor everything in existence as we align ourselves with the rest of the cosmos. When we practice this ceremonial Calendar, we offer our unconditional love with a simple thought or elaborate ceremony.

I welcome you to honor your Eternal Self, Past, Present, and Future lifetimes. Your Soul chose many incarnations eons ago, which has led you here. The names and symbols of the ancient glyphs or Nahuatl show us the exact journey of the road map. Using the Sacred Mayan calendars, we can reveal the codes of your incarnation stream.

I will help you relate to your mission, should you choose to accept it, and help you better connect to all of your corresponding helpers who are willing to assist you in accomplishing our mission. You can also draw and borrow from Past and Future lifetimes should you find yourself in a bind in this current incarnation.

It is immensely empowering to remember who you are at that Eternal level as each of us impacts the destiny of Humanity.

Our Ancient Future begins here. Will you step into it?

JOSE FEDERICO AJPU MUNOZ

ABOUT THE AUTHOR

Tata Jose is a Timekeeper, spiritual guide, and ceremonial leader of the Mayan Chor'Ti people and the spoken word of Mayan History from 1444 to 1529, which he calls the Northern Territories, which range from Guatemala to the west of Alaska and to the East of Montreal. Additionally, he is the carrier of the new

26,000-year Cycle Calendar known as the Sixth Sun Calendar, which started on December 22, 2012.

Tata Jose is a dream warrior and a crystal skull guardian. As mentioned in this Chapter, he can attest to crossing the stepping stones leading from Atl'antix towards the purple mountain.

In conjunction with the Mayan Calendar, he has been able to tap into his astrological signs or Nawals (Tzi Oc the Dog and the others) and begin the rediscoveries of his origins from Xibalba as well as his connections with his Starseed family from Michihuacan.

Tata Jose has dedicated his life to world peace. Since 1990, he has worked with several peace groups to raise awareness of the Mayan Calendar Destiny on the Path to 2036 as a Mayan Timekeeper.

To learn more about Jose's future-bending events or schedule a private Mayan Cosmology Reading, go to:

ManifestationStations.com

12

STARDUST BLOOD CODES

PATRICIA WALD-HOPKINS

Stardust Blood: Codes for Harmony on Earth

"*My story of the star lineage of my Cosmic Mother lineage"* is a channeled transmission from my higher self, accounting for the ancient star lineages that are coded in the mitochondrial DNA of my flesh and blood. My name is Patricia Librada Gallegos Wald-Hopkins. I am a modern mystic, author, and artist. My work in this lifetime is to share the wisdom of the stardust in my blood through my writing and art as a transformational lifestyle guide. We all hold sacred body wisdom from the stars in our blood, and my true desire is to inspire you to dive deep into the magic, power, and beauty of your own sacred stardust blood mystery -- so you too can share your cosmic mother star codes for a harmonious new Earth.

My Sacred Soul Mission

As I write this, I am almost 51 years old, but my awakening to my sacred soul mission began in earnest about 14 years ago.

Transmission

"I am here to be in service to Gaia Sophia by seeding harmony codes from the cosmos as I journey on Earth in this lifetime. I carry harmony codes that have been unlocked and activated within my own sacred body over my life through the trials of being human and by receiving the beauty and mystery frequencies of sacred places on Earth.

These are cosmic mother harmony codes and are divine codes of creation for the golden age of the new Earth. They are spoken into form through light language, my native tongue, and shared through art and the written word. In this incarnation at this time, it is my sole purpose to amplify this frequency of harmony throughout my entire sphere of influence here on Earth.

I am an interstellar architect and engineer of new earth designs. I am an intergalactic emissary and peacekeeper. It is my pleasure to share this story with you and activate the cosmic mother harmony creation codes of new Earth within your own body and consciousness so that you, too, may amplify the frequency throughout your sphere of influence in this lifetime.

Together we rise in the frequency of the harmony of the cosmic mother to create only from a place of cosmic equilibrium as we root out and recycle the energies of corruption that still exist within the old systems of patriarchal consciousness and form.

I go by many names and prefer to be felt and remembered as the whispers of sacred secrets in the wind, the cleansing sound of water, the rejuvenating smell of the Earth, the replenishing touch of rain, the delightful fragrance of the Rose, the warmth of the sun, the coolness of the moonlight and the starlight on your bare skin. I am a galactic time traveler and timeline keeper of the ancient consciousness of the Earth, who speaks the ancient languages of light and creation, and a priestess of Gaia Sophia. My first incarnation on Earth was Lemuria.

Blessed be the ones that walk as kings and queens of the Kingdoms of Light on Earth. Blessed be the light-workers reunited for the ascension of Gaia Sophia.

It is the time of unification and the time of the Great Change. I also carry the codes of mutation needed to alter the very structures of reality to open the portal for new forms of higher consciousness to land upon the desolate soils of our Mother Earth and make them fertile again.

Each of you carries a sacred seed of creation within you and aligning that with the frequency of cosmic mother harmony ensures that all shall prosper. Those that walk in harmony are the sacred gardeners and midwives of new life and the harmonic forms of beings to come. We may not be privy to most of them in this lifetime, but in our multidimensionality, we can imagine them and bring them down and into the core of Mother Earth, where they shall rise in divine time.

We are the Starseeds of tranquility, harmony, and peace lineages. Blessed be those that walk this path of service. I bow to you and celebrate your beautiful Essence and existence on this planet at this time for being here now to receive this activation."

Twelve Harmony Codes

There are 12 primary harmony codes of the cosmic mother that I will share here. They come from different star systems and sacred places on Earth. They are very much alive within my blood: Lyran, Arcturian, Pleiadian, Sirian, Lemurian, Atlantean, Egyptian, Tibetan, Nepalese, French, Spanish, and the North, Central & South American.

I carry these 12 codes in my blood and have activated them through deep contemplation and journey in multi-dimensional time travel's physical and non-physical nature. I have spent time visiting and communing with sacred lands and sites to activate codes there and receive additional activations that initiate the embodiment and sharing of the frequency transmissions with my sphere of influence and beyond in a multi-dimensional spectrum of light frequency shared; through teaching, writing, and art.

In this chapter, I briefly share the aspects that are most important at this time and ready to be received by the planet.*

Lyran

Lyran carries the divine union of the sacred feminine and sacred masculine rulership within a body. The primary code is that of the royal lineages of Lyra, the original leaders among humanoids. Leaders who lead with the heart's intelligence are implemented with the precision of the mind. The original blueprint of the king and queen before the distortion of the humanoid patriarchal codes, the mind virus of the advancing intellectual society as the prefrontal cortex was encouraged to grow beyond the original design for a harmonious relationship between love and logic.

It is time to clean and clear the personal and collective karmic cellular debris around leadership with love. To cleanse the cellular memory of the fear imprints that came with mind dominant living where the goal sought to save the one over the many where the one may be the one individual or the one group, community, country, etc. that considers itself to be the elite and therefore worthy of dominion. It is time to clear the corruption codes that distort the relationship between sacred masculine and feminine leadership to restore the harmonious flow of one to the other in holy matrimony and divine union.

Once again, it is about reactivating the original divine marriage blueprint and that of the divine family and creating the divine children's lineage upon Earth. The royal bloodline is one of justice for all, irrespective of origins. It is time to restore the cosmic timeline to the default of a harmonious relationship between the duality of the yin and the yang until it is the sacred one of unity consciousness.

Arcturian

The second code is the Arcturian heart song for the unconditional love and healing frequency of the original Arcturian civilization that allowed them to prosper. The anchoring of this code upon the Earth at this time infuses the crust and the core of Gaia with the frequency of joy, the universal celebration of life force at the basic cellular level. The joy of receiving the sunlight that kisses your skin. The basic joy of being a living and breathing being with no agenda for doing, where the only agenda is to emanate joy. Only a select few will take on this code, for it requires a life of non-doing, and the new Earth still needs the architects and the builders, so it will be only a small fraction of the humans that are the pure quintessential lovers.

Pleadian - Sirian

The third and fourth harmony codes come together as a pair

activation of the Pleiades - Sirius unity consciousness codes that will activate the advanced forms of living conditions through the transmissions of the advanced engineering and technology from these star nations.

Lemurian - Atlantean

The fifth and sixth harmony codes are also a pair unit activation of the Lemuria - Atlantis unity codes of heart and logic-based cultures on the original Earth to ensure that all advanced technologies developed on the new Earth are in the right relationship between heart and mind.

Egyptian

The seventh harmony code is the advanced Egyptian technology and sacred alchemy on Earth code. It represents the sacred union of the alchemist and the goddess. It is the reinfusion of the Earth grids with high magic and alchemy.

Nepalese - Tibetan

The eighth and ninth codes are also a pair unit activation which comprises Nepal/Tibet codes of strength and resilience of the Himalayas. About 20 years ago, I was in the Khumbu region of the Himalayas. I camped below a high mountain pass between Tibet and Nepal and struggled with extreme depletion and exhaustion. I didn't realize the significance of this event until many years later. I had been guided to this remote place to connect to and embody the energy of the sacred mountains and to retrieve the secret of the star geometry embedded in the rocks along with the memories of the ancient ones that lived there in communion with the star beings. My initiation was to be put to extreme physical trials in this place and imprinted with strength and resilience for this time of Great Change.

French - Spanish

The tenth and eleventh codes are a pair activation that comprises the France/ Spain Mary Magdalene and Yeshua teachings and the sacred geometry of the Andalusian lands of the Alhambra architecture to bring back the original codes of the Rose.

American

The final twelfth code is composed of the codes from the three Americas (North, Central, and South) and represents the indigenous wisdom of living in harmony with all of life.

A major part of my work here on Earth is to open up people to their multidimensional selves and guide them to be emissaries of sacred Earth, rising in their sacred leadership and as stewards of the resources of Gaia as they receive and integrate these 12 primary harmony codes. I do this using my Butterfly Healing Method™.

Butterfly Healing Method™

I mentor clients while holding them in the cosmic mother harmony frequency that bathes and saturates their cells with this energy allowing a shift in their biochemistry to be open to experience harmony on Earth. I use my Butterfly Healing Method™ to do this work. This method includes various Vibrational Therapies, Akashic Record Guidance, and Multidimensional Oracle Card Activations.

Vibrational Therapies include sound healing, light language activations, crystal therapy, energy healing, chakra balancing, Reiki, aromatherapy, and cranial-sacral therapy.

Multidimensional Oracle Card Activations are based on a codex of light that I developed through my art and contemplations to assist others in recognizing the key aspects of their multidimensional self, which includes cosmic, elemental, and higher self wisdom; as well as identifying which chakras need healing and balancing to activate and embody a client's unique multidimensional blueprint fully. I also use the codex to fully identify what karmic healing must be in your multi-dimensional power in this lifetime. The codex is a 55-card oracle deck published and available to my clients and the public.

Akashic Records Guidance is soul-level work to illuminate blocks to a client's soul mission, clear them, and implement new ways of being and doing through my inspired life coaching.

I also weave in Gene Keys Guidance as a sacred map of higher consciousness to support a client's process and elements of basic human design and astrology.

Closing Blessing

"We walk together now in the pure harmonic light of the Cosmic Mother, holding and emanating the vibration from our cells as we weave and amplify the codes of harmony on Earth. We are blessed to be of such service to Gaia Sophia and the Cosmic Mother. So blessed and filled with gratitude, and so it is."

Thank you for receiving this transmission.

PATRICIA WALD-HOPKINS

ABOUT THE AUTHOR

Patricia Wald-Hopkins is a Modern Mystic, Infinite Self Catalyst, and Soul Liberation Guide for those ready to break free from old paradigm limitations and awaken to the gifts of their Infinite Self, so they can lead the life they are DIVINELY designed to live. She supports her clients as an Akashic Records Wisdom Guide and with various healing and transformational modalities, including essential oil perfumes, crystals, and light language to support them to embody their Infinite Self. She is a Gene Keys Ambassador and Guide and a co-founder of the School of Light, a mystery school based on Gene Keys transmission. She is the author of a chapter, The EmBODY Codes: Transmissions of a Mystic on the Sacred Body and Being Human, in the book Sacred Body Wisdom: Igniting the Flame of Our Divine Humanity; the author of the chapter, The Miracle of Light Language: Awakening to My Soul Voice and Purpose, in the book Miraculous, and the creator of the Infinite Self Oracle Card deck.

Patriciawaldhopkins.com

13

EMPATH'S KEY TO TRANSFORMATION

BY: HJALTI FREYR KRISTINSSON

He walked into the room. I felt stressed and unsure why, but I did. Felt my body tense up, shorter breath! What was I doing wrong? I didn't know that I had done anything wrong. Everything was just fine a few moments ago. Now, I felt totally out of place. My co-worker, who had just walked in, began criticizing my work, even though it was not his assignment to work with. After a minute or two, he got out of the room. Wow, that was strange! Things calmed quite fast. What was that? Things got back to normal. I kept on working and felt good. Then suddenly, my co-worker came back into the room again, and now, what? My body got triggered and jumped up with intensity, and my muscles contracted. And no, it was not because I was startled by his sudden abruptness, like when someone sneaks up at you and tries to scare you, but with the strange observation of realizing that my whole system was reacting so super sensitively to my co-worker's own stress, and very negative state of being at that time. He had been having some problems in his life, and his way of dealing with them seemed to convey his unbalanced feelings to everyone around him. Not that he ever attacked me directly, but this was quite an obvious pattern for everyone to see. I knew this was just how he was, but my bodily system could not help but automatically react this time. And with that, this dear co-worker became one of my greatest teachers. Well, regarding this focused teaching at that moment, his being had shown me a VERY direct way how my system automatically reacted when he pressed my 'Button On.' And then 'On again' sending waves of energetic discomfort, making my body nervously jump up and down, along with a strong surge of stress and anger, which I finally realized was not mine.

This over-exaggerated reaction in myself around his energy helped me finally realize on a much deeper level how my body and energy functioned, which supported me in my own awakening of self-awareness.

I began to understand my subtle sensitivities to the feelings of some people around me. I understood better that I can feel so much, feeling all kinds of emotions such as worries, anxiety, anger, despair, exhaustion, fatigue, and overthinking that cause more problems, along with all kinds of other feelings (thankfully, some positive ones too), but still. And yes, some of those feelings were my own, but the majority, where did that come from? With my rising awareness at the time, I began to realize, discover and identify many of those feelings were not actually from me.

As I was attracted more and more to meditation, I was now set on a new vibrational path to discover what was my own true energy and feelings. To reach a deeper level of relaxation in a meditative state to where I could feel and experience my own true energy and feelings without the distractions (at least on a much deeper level than before). I became better and better at just being me, feeling me, my *"I am"*, being in my own energy and recognizing it as me, which also led to more fine tuning of my ability to distinguish and recognize the stuff I was picking up from the 'outside.'

I had unknowingly been subconsciously taking other people's negative emotions around me ever since I can remember making them my own and therefore taking responsibility for solving them. Saying yes to everyone when asked for help, whether it was an honest request or just someone who didn't feel like being responsible for themselves or just being too lazy to do their own 'chore.' I had become the automatic someone for help, the go-to guy. And mostly for all the wrong reasons, because I always felt obliged to, because I always felt the problem within myself, which I wanted to solve, to feel better. Until now, I finally discovered how I was automatically reacting to all the problems of others and realized they were not mine to solve. I finally allowed myself to dig deeper into discovering myself, my problems, and my own needs and wishes. What did I really want? Who I really was.

Meditation and self-reflection have always been a big part of my life. Being aware of something more than what we can 'see' with various spiritual experiences and knowledge under my belt, I used meditation as my gateway to learning more about myself, to get close to the clearer version of me, the I AM in me. With that, I discovered my own right to be how I AM, and how I AM in my own full right to be in balance and at ease, to feel happy, to feel I have complete dominance over my own energy. I learned to better recognize when various feelings and conflicts from others were trying to invade my space. Since I was learning more about where and what my pure energy was, it was much easier to recognize what is me and what is not me.

And therefore, I could set the boundaries of not allowing

just everything to come into my own energy as my own. But to recognize this means having actual decision power to block it or explore it further alongside discovering more of my own energy. And now, when I had awakened to discover my own energy in a much stronger and focused way, I was able to put my focus and attention on what I wanted, what issues I had for myself that I wanted to work with, and where I wanted to go in life, what I wanted to be and dedicate my life to, and get a much deeper connection to why I AM here, now. Everything changed for me. When I stepped into my own power.

This was, of course, just one of many lessons I went through on my own journey through life, as if I'm going through a practical school of enlightenment, according to the pre-planned order in the custom-made program I created for myself before coming here. Rings a bell?

Later on, I learned the concept of 'empaths' and how many others struggle with similar things I have been going through. While I was first discovering this for myself, I had been inclined to learn all types of healing methods. I even learned massage therapy, implemented my healing work, learned various meditations and began working with energy, senses, intuition, and the deeper levels of consciousness.

I had begun studying this side of life quite young, 'me.' I was a very calm, shy, introverted, and super-sensitive kid, always in the background, doing my best to cope with the world around me. Even when bullied at school as a youngster and teenager, I managed to stay afloat by studying the energy and behavioral patterns of those around me (especially my classmates who often fell into their own self-protecting mode as bullies) and doing something popular (even acting as a DJ) and a lot of preventive measures by recognizing their patterns (by feeling and easy logic). When other teenagers my age were busy partying and socializing, I was studying auras, energies, meditation, spirituality, aliens, dimensions, enlightenment, etc. It became very natural for me, but at the same time, I noticed how often isolating this was as I could only talk to the much older people about my interests which was fine by me, being the introvert I was. But, I also noticed that so many people were having similar problems as me, sensing all kinds of things, day or night, some also waking up and during the night, feeling paralyzed, or sensing something close to them, not knowing what it was or what to do about it. With fear as the usual number one winner when experiencing something unknown, I began to assist people in realizing there are other ways as well. Instead of automatically being afraid of something they don't understand, maybe approach it more with curiosity and calmness. If you really can contain the usual fear to come out when something 'strange' is happening, how about looking at it as something worth exploring, to understand it better, to see what is really going on (up to the point that your brain allows you to understand at that moment). When you feel being touched gently on the shoulder, do you instantly jump up with full armor and sword to attack back, or can you invite the possibility of being 'touched' by a loved one, angel, or spiritual guide, trying to let you know they are with you, watching over you? When you hear a sudden noise around you (something you feel is not from the physical realm), can you invite the possibility of being signaled from something well-intentioned instead of something to be automatically afraid of? When you sense something that might even appear frightful, could it be another way of communicating with someone well-intending?

With stronger inner calmness and a closer connection to

yourself, you become much more capable of approaching everything with higher awareness and have a broader range of possibilities, of discovering and understanding things for what they really are, instead of something that our brain tries to connect it with automatically, based on previous conditioning (by ourselves or our environment). When you train yourself to be able to keep calm and centered, connected to your own center, your own core of being, daily, your awareness of yourself and things around you are raising up everything in your own vibration, your physical and energy body, in your broadcast within and your broadcast to the world around you. Like how the micro-particles in water change their form in coherence with the influencing frequency nearby, we do the same in our bodies. But, unlike water, you can control the frequency you are vibrating. And you can control the frequency you are broadcasting outwards. It's easier than you might think. But first, let's focus on how you are sensing yourself.

Do you feel a difference in yourself when you feel calm, at ease, and in balance, rather than when you feel stressed, tired, drained, and out of control? Yes, of course.

Do you feel the difference when looking at the color red and the color blue? Yes, most likely.

Do you feel the difference while listening to the rhythmic beat of the native American drum and the synthesizer-generated techno drum beat? Yes, most likely.

Do you feel the difference between sitting in the forest with beautiful harmonic sounds of nature around you or experiencing the heavy loudness and raw power of thunderstorms? Yes, most likely.

Do you feel the difference when you talk to someone heart to heart, a glowing and nourishing communication, or when someone is attacking you verbally or behaving narcissistically towards you? Yes, definitely.

Do you feel the difference within you when you are totally at peace, in balance, and centered instead of when you are not? Yes, most likely. But it can sometimes be challenging to be aware of it throughout the day.

Do you feel the difference when you are tired, low, exhausted by physical work, and when you feel something invading your space, something not doing you good, something draining, something unusually stressful, something dark, something with roots outside your own energy? Yes, you might, but it can often be much harder to identify.

As you can see, there are many layers of what all of us are feeling every day, and all of us have different and unique versions of it, being the unique beings each one of us is, and yes, you too.

But all of us have this thing in common. *"WE FEEL THINGS."*

Some get more startled than others. Some feel deeper feelings than others. Some feel and sense more colorful experience than others. Some even try to block out all they feel when it gets too much.

We all feel. And it is up to us to decide how to deal with it, how well we understand it, to either allow it to control us or be our guidance and a way to help us understand and possibly live our lives more richly.

Instead of letting ourselves be controlled by how we feel, by fear, by anger, by not knowing, by craving more energy in whatever form, by thinking we are not enough, or lacking something, not being perfect, and this and that and everything in between, how about we connect with the unlimited source of love within, every day, and that way remind ourselves that we really have a connection to everything we really need to achieve what we truly want (whether we realize it at each time or not). Yes, we may want many things, but what do we truly need?

How would your life be different if you connected daily to your own perfect, true state, inner power, the true source of universal love, and connection to your I AM being. Further, how would you feel about maintaining awareness of yourself, your daily tasks, chores, projects, feelings, inspirations, relationships, your current vibration, goals, visions, life journey, discoveries of enlightenment, and your heightening frequency levels?

There are so many wonderful healing modalities out there, being done by so many wonderful beings, each excelling in their unique approach to helping people heal and transform their lives. At the beginning of my massage/healing practice, my focus was always to create a pathway for people to reach a deeper level of relaxation. The kind of depth where people are usually sleeping, but with my hands-on massage work, I kept them usually in a conscious, awake state at the same time their body was in a deep sleep, enabling them to feel a clear state of being, which opened their conscious connection to their own inner balance, harmony, healing and so much more. Of course, I was also in constant self-learning how things worked, got more developed and intuitively reaching deeper, higher, more perspectives, deeper relations with higher frequencies, but also realizing more and more that instead of me being the 'healer,' I was there to help people ignite their own self-healing, to help them reach their own deeper level to resolve whatever they were dealing with. It became even more obvious when I later added on various kinds of hypnosis and coaching, alongside various training and seminars I had done for people, that there are so many ways to ignite their own glow, inspiration, and connection to their own center of being--their own source of universal love.

I had finally found my way, as a technically-inclined introverted empath, where I used my journey of lessons and discoveries to assist others in their own journey. I am humbled to be of service to those who seek my assistance on their way to their own path to the next phase of enlightenment.

In love and light,

Hjalti Freyr Kristinsson (aka Kris)

SAYING:

“Empathy is a special way of coming to know another and yourself.”
- Carl R. Rogers

HJALTI FREYR KRISTINSSON

ABOUT THE AUTHOR

From a young age, Hjalti has always been an eager student of self-development, healing & consciousness, and technically inclined. Starting early on, he practiced the arts of intuition, meditation, and various healing methods. He mixed deep relaxation with various energy work, helping people to discover new connections to themselves. Hjalti became a licensed massage therapist, adding deep-relaxation methods with various energy work.

In 2004 Hjalti became a Silva UltraMind ESP instructor, offering events assisting people in discovering more of their own mind's potential. As an ever-learning student, Hjalti also studied and practiced various meditations and spiritual consciousness, licensed hypnotherapy, and QHHT. It further led Hjalti to become a certified ICF Coach, which he then has combined with his intuitive approach to ignite a deeper connection for people within themselves. Hjalti offers personal sessions, lectures, and seminars and is currently publishing online programs focused on improving people's lives with higher awareness and meditation, with a special focus on empaths and energy workers.

Hjalti's home country is Iceland, but in 2020 he moved with his family to Spain, where they currently live, and Hjalti keeps on doing his services locally & globally via the internet.

Hjalti F. Kristinsson (aka Kris)
hjaltikristinsson.com

14

DREAMING DOLPHINS

AROS CRYSTOS

Working with the Dolphins

My work with the dolphins for the last 30 years has taught me how to approach life from a multidimensional level, which opens up all sorts of possibilities. How can you and I hold in our consciousness a future that includes all humanity, species, and other galaxies? It is certainly not for the once clinging to limitations, such as families, traditions, beliefs, and concepts about everything and everyone. If I want to create a future that serves and honors all of this creation, I must live in the moment to dream about the future because I have been programmed to see and strive for the future from the old paradigm. My humble understanding is that the human consciousness has been limited to the perception that we are limited and can only achieve certain knowledge from an educational point of view, making us subject to not trust in our innate abilities. There must be a balance between the mind and the heart. My divine self is mirrored in that reflection as a bright crystal when the intellect is purified. How can I possibly achieve such a beautiful state of being?

Simplicity vs. Technology

Simplicity, and instead of going forward with fast-moving-unknown technology. Bring yourself back to the center of your being and start from there. Who am I? No matter how much-advancement technology provides, without asking this question and being willing to let that be the guiding beacon, I am going nowhere, and I will be guided by everything except my divine being. I understand that this might often not be sophisticated enough and too simple, and therein lies the problem. My interactions with the dolphins have taught me to approach my life with a sense of humor and lightness of being. Observing them and interacting with them, they make a simple leaf game powerful teaching and a reminder of what is important. The masters share with us, *"Become childlike and spontaneous again,"* not childish, a vast difference. As so-called grown-ups, we have substituted our innate intelligence with learned and programmed behavior, and anything that goes against that must be avoided at any cost.

A childlike state is a very advanced state of consciousness because it originates from the core of our being, where life again becomes a wonder of rediscovery. People look for miracles as a signpost. The irony is that they completely forget the greatest miracle of all. Being alive in this body and experiencing life itself is a miracle. In a childlike state, our hearts are open to the wonder of an existence beyond the five physical senses. We start recognizing that we are fully alive and experiencing a wondrous adventure where all things are possible, and nothing is impossible. Yet! We are empowered to shun such nonsense, focus on what is important, and become responsible human beings, a product of the systems that decide what you can think, believe, and act upon. First, I must understand that this is happening, which allows me to ask again, who am I? It brings you out of the system and opens your heart and mind to expand and embrace a different reality to see your life and circumstances. Now, let's dream of the future filled with all of the heart's longings, and in that place, there is no limit to what we can create together.

Dolphin Pod Consciousness

Another teaching from the dolphins how to dream into the future and a holistic approach to life is dolphin pod consciousness. Being that this is about Starseeds and their understanding of life, let's include here all our brothers and sisters from various star systems and planets and galaxies and be in the clear understanding that we were never alone on this adventure and, at the same time, we came here to gain more understanding about life in the third dimension as it all counts to our future explorations and deeper longing to realize we are still infants on this journey. Life as a holistic journey is the soil we must cultivate in our consciousness and make sure we plant the most beautiful and transformative thoughts that will grow to become a kingdom within a kingdom.

Dolphin's Unity Consciousness

I have always felt that humans are operating from a reverse

mirror effect. Dolphins live and interact from unity consciousness, and at the same time, they are unique and different in their expression and behavior. It becomes so clear in their movement in the water when they create a pattern of sacred geometry that can only be achieved in unity consciousness. For example, when people try to hide behind a mask, it becomes obvious what they are hiding. On the other hand, a transparent and open individual cannot be put in a box as he acts from a place of freedom. Since the dolphins are traveling in and out of different dimensions within the ocean's womb, it's evident that the ocean is not what we have been led to believe. Yes, it is a water element, of course, and we have many species to be found there. The oceans are a multidimensional vortex with portals available to dolphins and humans once they raise their consciousness. Mother Earth is a divine jewel among planets and stars. She has all the answers to every question and will reveal it to those who honor and respect her entire being with all its inhabitants. In my opinion, we do not need to explore space. We must understand that the Universe starts inside Mother Earth and her oceans and within ourselves to access other dimensions. There is a specific reason why Starseeds have come here to understand that the body they occupy is mostly made out of the water element. Our planet is covered in 2/3 of water, and there are not too many water-occupied planets in this part of the galaxy.

Inner work

Being a Starseed takes huge responsibility and understanding. The simple truth is that all dimensions are entwined like threads in a garment. You can never leave something that is part of you. You can transcend it and live from that place. There's nothing wrong with the idea, *"We will ascend to a higher plane of consciousness,"* but it's an internal job. If you don't look within and work on yourself, it keeps all of us in a spin. You are already everything you are looking for. Just awake to your true divine nature. There is no place to go or come from. You are always a divine multidimensional being, which we are all here to remember. The answer is not looking up into the sky and searching for our star families among the stars or in their ships. Remember simplicity!

"Look within and recognize yourself as everyone and everything, and at that moment, you may just see thousands of ships waiting for you and many other wonders."

As humans, we tend to look where it cannot be found. It's like the man looking for some coins he had lost on the ground, in the dark, without any light to guide him. Sounds silly, right? Yet this is exactly what many of us are still doing. We have a real challenge to grasp that we are truly divine with all the answers within ourselves. As Starseeds, you are a role model for what is possible and be an example of living in star nations and living from a higher consciousness. Again the more light you carry, the more responsibility you have for that light. You must be vigilant, respect and honor human conditioning without getting caught up in it or trapped. You signed on the dotted line before coming here, and now it's high noon to complete and fulfill your work here. Dream!

Dream Big and Grandiose

Dream of an empire of untold possibilities. Being a

Chulosians from the planet Chulos in the Vega star system is part of my heritage. These beings are half dolphins and half-humans. Their upper body is dolphin and then from the waist human. They are mentioned in the book by Robert Temple, The Sirius Mystery, and how they visited the Dogon tribe in Africa and shared the wisdom that the Dogons have documented. How I found out was quite simple. I was giving a seminar about the dolphins and shared about the Dogons, and then a few weeks later, I was in Sedona working, and a man gave me this drawing of the Chulosians. He said, I am to give this to you, and then the next moment, by another person, I was given a book, not available officially, written by a man from Nasa that used to have top clearance about how the Chulosians had visited Earth by the north pole and had gathered heads of states to meet with them to share with them -- that there was a portal that could be accessed to another dimension. They left as they felt we were not ready for this information.

It is something that Starseeds must recognize that most of humanity at this time is not ready for certain teachings and part of our work is to prepare the ones ready we come in contact with. It is a way that they feel respected and honored and empowered to trust in themselves again.

A holistic future must start with the right approach and understanding. This approach must be planted in the minds as a changed vocabulary and heightened awareness. In other words, we must truly understand that we are responsible for every thought and action. There are no random thoughts as such. Also included in this is the awareness that the *"Truth can only be digested in bits and pieces,"* and the dilemma currently on this planet is that :

"The information highway has too many lanes and moving too fast to

be able to absorb all of these overloads of information and to be able to detract the valid ones."

Everybody seems to feel they know and want to share this information with the planet and everyone on it. The one who thinks he knows may know not. I concluded that I know now enough to realize I do not know everything, and there is such freedom as it feels like a heavy burden has been lifted. Imagine all that information and carrying that around with you inside and outside. The mind can be imagined as a giant garbage can. If you do not empty it, it will start to smell.

Similarly, if I do not empty my mind, I will become more and more stressed and lose sight of my intentions and purpose. The dolphins and their consciousness are a brilliant mirror of what we must return to. When they asked me to be one of their ambassadors on the planet, I thought, now I get to interact with them all the time in the open oceans. Quite the opposite, interact with them for a while, and then they would clearly state, time for you to leave and share our information with humans on land. For almost the last thirty years being in this position as an ambassador, I had to let go of most of my ideas and concepts and embrace a different way of interacting and sharing the teachings of the dolphins. Countless times I have heard that we are feeling the dolphins all around us, and some saw dolphins swimming in my energy field, and for certain, their intelligence has made sure the teachings have been delivered with spontaneity and laughter. It has also served me well as a practice:

"To let go more and more of my limiting beliefs about myself and almost everything and everyone."

So I feel I am qualified to share how to dream of a holistic future into reality where we have no more struggles. I want to think that everyone is practicing living from the heart and following that tiny whisper within where the money system is something of the past. People are loved and respected for no particular reason, except they are divine multidimensional beings and have the power and right understanding to dream anything they choose to as long as it benefits everyone. Then as a Starseed, you are fulfilling your role here. As a Starseed, you are the combination of many star beings. We are energy and various vibrations of frequencies that determine who we are. You must also thank yourself for your service and acknowledge that you are great. The ego sometimes does not allow that to happen. It tells you, you are selfish! When I can acknowledge small things during the day, I train myself to acknowledge my true nature. Yes, you are great! Never diminish yourself or your work, no matter what it is. All work can be important if I change my attitude around it. So I will complete my sharing of who you and I are beyond any description and accomplishment, even service. Rest in that awareness, do your best, and surrender the result to your divine self.

AROS CRYSTOS

ABOUT THE AUTHOR

Aros Crystos is an author, artist, avid traveler and seeker of truth who have been on spiritual path to awaken people in rediscovering their divine multidimensional selves. Born on April 10, 1947, in a small town in southern Sweden, he lived in Germany, London, Spain, other parts of Europe, India, and the United States.

At the airport in Los Angeles, all his identification with his old life disappeared, all his belongings was stolen, and his last connection with the identity of who he used to be, gone. He renounced his old life, trading high society in Europe for the vast longing to live in the moment. It led him to his meditation teacher and mentor, Baba Muktananda, and his successor Gurumayi.

Living in Hawaii, Aros began to receive communications from the realm of the ocean, leading him to spend years interacting with dolphins and whales in Hawai'i. At the same time, his galactic family began communicating with him again, just as when he was a child. His multi-dimensional soul began receiving profound, beautiful, and transformative messages through these interactions. He activates people through galactic vibrations coming through his vocal cords as a life coach and spiritual guide sought after by people of all walks of life. Aros share his knowledge to prepare people towards the next paradigm shift.

Find Aros at: Aros.life

15

EAGLE MEDICINE

BY: SARAH EAGLEWOMAN

The human spirit has been greatly affected by our over use of technology and society's addiction to social media culture. It's out of balance to where we become like robots. It disconnects us from reality, living from the core of our essence from our true authentic selves, our soul.

There's too much information that we're experiencing from the outside world that it becomes numbing. It shuts down what is going on in our internal world, our intuition, our soul communication. We lose touch with our spirit. We lose touch with the Creator. That's why it's important to sustain a daily practice through meditation, through breath medicine so you connect up! Because when you lose that connection, as the Grandmothers say, that's when disease can come through. Disease of the mind, body, spirit comes when there's a disconnection to the Creator.

—

It's about creating a connection with Creator, with source, with maker, whatever name you'd like to place on it. It's Supreme consciousness. The Supreme consciousness is the terminology I use to connect up to the Creator. I always say, *"Connect up to Creator, Creation, to Maker".* The Creator creation connection means being at one with source and drawing from the infinite well. You're drawing from this well and if you've got too many other things outside of you that's distracting you from this connection, then the soul becomes suppressed. That's when people say, *'I feel depressed, I feel anxious'* because they've lost the connection to Maker, the supreme consciousness.

We need something to look forward to! If we can just adjust our thinking and our way of looking at things, our perception, That is the key! The Eagles' perception is looking beyond what we know. Like I say, *"Forget what, you know and remember what you forgot".* You look beyond what you know. Life is not meant to be a regiment. It's discovering the newness each day, that thing to look forward to! Your everyday situation and circumstance allows you the opportunity to open up and discover a miracle, a life of transformation. Looking forward to something each day is important. Take the time to walk and discover, find the miracles and the little blessings that come along your path.

But, before you do that, before you set out into the world, it's important to create a ritual. It's important to even create a ceremony of protection, of divine guidance. You definitely want to connect up and ask; *"Please guide my thoughts, guide my path, guide my way so that I may see all the miracles that you bring forth to me and that I may be an instrument of your love, of your light. That I may know, with discernment, what it is that I'm supposed to do for all those that enter in my pathway."*

—

My Journey Walking the Shaman Eagle Medicine Path

I was born into it. I am a fifth-generation Medicine Woman and Shaman. I came into the world with the gifts of being able to see beyond the physical and the ability to heal.

It runs through my blood on both sides of my family. I'm a descendant of Geronimo, the great Apache Warrior Shaman. He was my great-great-uncle, and my great-great-grandmother was his sister. My great-grandmother was a healer, my grandmother could prophecies, and she was a hands-on healer. My mother, uncle, and siblings also had gifts. She chose not to pursue a life as a practicing medicine person. However, one of my uncles did. On my father's side, we are Toltec. His mother, my grandmother, was also a very gifted seer. I am honored to carry on the legacy on both sides.

As a child, I could see beyond the physical and hear from the spirit world, which I didn't understand at a very young age. I would hear voices with strong messages from the spirit realm, and it frightened me.

When I was three years old, my mother would come into my room, and I would be sitting and speaking jibber jabber in the corner. My Mother asked, *"Who are you talking to?"* In my little voice, I said, *'Blue lady!'* And I would point to the corner. My mother called up her brother, my uncle, a medicine man who became my teacher. She told him that I was talking to someone, but she didn't know who it was, just that I would point and say, *'Blue lady!'* My uncle told my mom to take me to the Catholic church and added, *"I feel I know who it is. Just walk in and see what she does and who she points to."* That day my mother took me to a Catholic church. I looked around the beautiful, big cathedral and walked right up to Mother Mary. In fact, I pointed to her and said, *'Blue lady,'* just like that. My mother knew that I was speaking to Mother Mary from then on. My mom took my hand, and I looked around the church in awe of the saints and the icons. Then we walked out of the church, and she took me for ice cream, my favorite! Throughout my life, Mother Mary has been one of the strong teachers and guardians who presides over me and often comes in with guidance when I'm working.

Up to this point, I thought that everybody could see like I could see or could hear what I was hearing, being clairvoyant and clairaudient. But I learned that wasn't the case.

I became more aware of these gifts and the extrasensory abilities at about 11 years old. Yet, I wanted to just be a teenager. I wanted to fit in. It was lonely. I didn't go out much because I was constantly trying to discern what I was experiencing. I still did not understand my gifts as a teenager. I suppose I was feeling and seeing things differently than others, what most people saw. I was trying to adjust and assimilate these gifts into my daily life. I just knew things, and every now and then, I would share it with whom I thought were my friends, but they too would make fun of me. They didn't understand my abilities. I would tell them certain things that would happen to them, not in a bad way, never out of any malice. It was simply obvious to me. The kids at school would say things about me like, *"She's a real strange one, what is she staring at?"* The girls would tease me about my abilities and would call me names. I never said, *"This is what I can do, this is what I can see."* They would always think I was very odd. Once in a while, I would tell them things that would blow them away or show them what was to come. For instance, I told a classmate, *"I see a woman standing by you and she says she's your grandmother and wants to tell you that she sees you and to not be sad that she left, she will always be there for you!"* When it came true, or they could see that I was right, some of them would turn white as a ghost! They were so shocked and would ask, *"How did you know that?"* They would get so scared, but my intention was purely innocent and meant to help. Because of their fear of me, they started to call me even more names; weirdo, alien from another planet, stuff like that. Being very shy didn't help. Sometimes I would go home and cry because of being so misunderstood and made fun of. My mom would say to me, *"Okay, well, not everyone has your gifts, the reason that they make fun of you is because they fear what they don't know and it scares them."* It gave me some confidence when she told me this, and I thought, *'Okay, now I understand my power.'*

Even with the girls acting mean, somehow, I could sense that their souls had a higher knowing and were trying to connect with mine. Unspokenly they were asking for my guidance and giving their permission. I answered by sharing what I was shown about them, but I was still discerning how or what I shared. Even then, without really understanding it, I was starting to live my purpose as a healer, to help people beyond their own personality traits that would try to intervene or interfere.

When I was about 13, my Mother's brother called and said to bring Sara to see me. He sat me down and said, *"It's time that you know the ways of our people because one day you are going to carry on the ways of our ancestors as a Medicine Woman. You will be the one to carry on the traditional ways."* He began to teach me and show me these ways. It wasn't until I was sent to study with my uncle that I truly began to understand who I am and what I carry. He taught me so much about my gifts and what he learned throughout his years as a Shaman Medicine Man.

One day, I remember running home from school being chased by demons. I'll never forget it. I could hear their voices. They were saying hellish things! It was so demonic, a lot of dark things being said. I knew they were demons at that moment because of how they were speaking to me. I ran all the way home, and I ran into the house. I ran past my mother and locked myself in my room. She ran in after me and said, *"What's wrong?"* Mother was really scared, she thought something really awful had happened to me like somebody hurt me. I finally opened the door, and I told her, *"I'm hearing these demonic voices."* She said, *"What do you mean?"* I said, *"They are saying these horrific things, and it's awful. I don't know what to do? They won't stop bothering me!"*

She would always call my uncle to explain and help me with what I was going through. My uncle said, *"Ahhh, she's important! That's why they're after her! Because of her gifts."* He told my mother, *"We've got to help her understand this so that she doesn't buy into what they have to say and get hurt."* He began to teach me. He said, *"Oh, they're chasing you because you have something to give that is very, very strong. You're going to give it to the world, and you're going to help many people, and they're trying to trip you up."* I said, *"Oh, thank you for sharing that, but what do I do so they don't come back?"* He said, *"Well, just me telling you, it will help you understand your gifts. You'll know to just tell them, hey, leave me alone! Stand back, move away!"* He continued to say: *"They see you have the ability to transform them. You have the warrior within you, that warrior spirit that comes through our lineage. We are warriors, and you will be a strong medicine woman, strong Shaman one day."* I was confronted by the demons because back then, little did I know that I was being prepared for the journey of becoming a Shaman. I was being initiated but not knowing at the time that's what was happening. That's when I started developing my protection tactics and practices. I still didn't really know what a Shaman meant, but my uncle told me not to research and just try to find out, let it come to me, and that he will help guide my way.

In high school, I became very much in tune with people's energy. Every year it seemed like it got stronger. I'd be sitting next to a person, and I would not feel good in my stomach. This happened often. I started to feel worse. I went to my mom, and I told her I thought I had cancer. She says, '*What?*'

I would tell her I heard a voice that said, "*You've got cancer.*" She took me to the doctor numerous times. This was our family doctor who knew me well. I was in and out of his office. He would say, "*Now, what do you have?*" And I would say, "*I think I have tuberculosis.*" And he would say, "*You can't even say the word. Now let's check you.*" He would say, "*You don't have that. Nor do you have cancer.*" I would say, "*I just feel these diseases.*" And he would say, "*Well, you don't have these diseases.*" He would tell me, "*You have got to stop this. You're being a hypochondriac.*"

My Mother asked my uncle why I was feeling everybody's sicknesses? He said it's because she's an empathic healer, and she's really in training. He went on to say the elders, the ancestors, are really getting her ready. They are teaching her not to take on the energy of illness but to understand it and transform it. My uncle told me, "*I would help many people with their illnesses. You'll discover that you have this ability to heal people from the deep soul level, where disease starts.*" So this was my training. I began to learn how to ground myself and understand how to be an empathic healer.

When I got older, I was initiated into my medicine and called on to receive my name, Eaglewoman. I showed my mother and my uncle my eagle feather. My uncle was quiet for a little bit. Then he finally spoke and said, "*You're the one who will carry on the traditional ways in our family.*" I cried, and my mom cried and said, "*No, I don't want her to!*" My uncle told her, "*This is her purpose. This is her calling.*" And my mom kept on crying. And she said, "*No, I don't want her to have to carry this! She's going to have to go through so much sacrifice, and it's too much for her to do."* And he said, *"No, it's not too much. It's what she's supposed to be doing. It's her calling. It's her gift. This is her purpose. She'll be protected and taken care of." My mom said, "It's just too much responsibility for her."*

My mother feared that it would be too much for me to take it on and it would interfere with my life. When you have a purpose of being responsible for the world's consciousness and humanity, it's scary for a parent. I'm sure Mother Mary said the same thing to Jesus! As I continued on in my Shaman Medicine practice, my Mother could see my strength and the positive impact of my abilities. She is proud of me. She became very supportive of my work. *'Wow!'* She would say! She would brag about me. *"My daughter is a Shaman. Did you know? My daughter is a Shaman."* She would tell anyone and everyone who would listen, and I am most grateful to my uncle and my Mother for seeing me, seeing who I am, and holding me in the light.

Eagle Medicine & Walking The Red Road

How you perceive your walk here on earth is so important. It directly affects how you experience your life. I was counseling a client about this, and as I listened to them speaking, I asked, did you hear yourself say, *'Everyone?'* Well, you're not thinking this way; you're different! I'm different! And where two or more are gathered, we can conquer that perception of *"Everyone is thinking this way"* and make the change. You have to discover that there must be someone, such as myself, who is not in that flow or in that group. So right there, that was a perfect example of how the majority of people out in the world will group and say, *'Everyone'* instead of saying, *"Well, there are some."* I advised my client that it was important they change their perception and how they were speaking to it and looking at it. How? By walking the Red Road.

Walking the red road is a practice of confronting your fears with discipline and a higher light of understanding. Go beyond the mundane and be fearless as you walk outside your comfort zone. Becoming a manifestor of your own life takes courage, excitement, and curiosity. It is innate to be guided by your soul. You gain that connection through spiritual practice. As the great Yeshua and the great Masters say, *"The healing always begins with you, you want to see a change, you be the change."* So if enough of us can be the change, then before you know it, we've defeated the naysayers, the depression and sadness, and even the negativity within ourselves. There's a diffusion taking place. As long as you don't resonate or align yourself with someone else's thought process. Because then before you know it, you're thinking like them and saying what's the use. Then you've submitted, your suppressed, depressed, and can't move forward because now you've joined them. So, it all begins with you!

To carry Eagle Medicine is a big responsibility. I must always see things from the highest, purest perception, an Eagles perception. Remain free from any judgment or criticism, so I can help to guide and heal people with discernment. It is my responsibility to connect up to the Creator's vision and anchor it through, as above, so below, and do so in an honorable way, with integrity. I call it the light of understanding. This is what it means to *"Walk the Red Road,"* to walk this journey through life with courage, purpose, dignity, and humbleness. Aho!

I wish you many blessings,
I bless you with my love,
Eaglewoman

~

SAYING:

"As soon as healing takes place, go out and heal somebody else."

— Maya Angelou

SARA EAGLEWOMAN

ABOUT THE AUTHOR

Known worldwide as the Urban Shaman, ***Sara Eaglewoman*** is a Doctor of the Soul. She is a descendant of Geronimo, the great Apache Warrior Shaman. For over three decades, she has been a practicing Medicine Woman in the art of Indigenous, Shamanic, and Intuitive Healing. Her work realigns and redesigns the road map of your soul, bringing forth the highest alignment and wealth of the body, mind, and soul. Ealgewoman brings her gifts to the trenches of today's society and one's own personal challenges, needs, and goals. The Eagle Medicine ways are a quickening of change on a core soul level. An uprooting of all that is being presented that wants to shift, heal and transmute at that time.

Eaglewoman transforms your life by changing the *'Outcome'* to *'Become.'* As an intuitive healer, life counselor, spiritual guide, and consultant to Fortune 500 leaders of the industry, celebrities, musicians, politicians, people of all ages and all walks of life, she divinely guided healing and counsel are highly sought after and regarded as sacred realignment work of the soul. Whether helping people through major life changes or challenges, assisting those with illness to heal or to cross, she lays out a new pathway for one to travel on. As a bridge to the multi-dimensions, Eaglewoman guides and aligns people to their healing and successes to that next level of expansion and self-realization.

For more information go to:
www.eaglewoman.com

16

UNITY

BY: JASON SHURKA

The Future of Humanity

My name is Jason Shurka, but who *I AM* is a whole different story. What you are about to read is intended to inspire you, as the reader, to be your greatest and highest self. On the surface, we can all list tons of things we *'Do,'* but is that what really matters? Let me show you what I mean. I'm an author, I'm a visionary, I'm a businessman, I'm a healer, I'm a creator, but who am I really? I told you what I *'Do,'* yet you still have no idea who I am. So, let me simplify one of the most fundamental truths. I am you, and you are me. We may *'Do'* different things, and we may look different, but all in all, we are connected to the same divine intelligence that makes our heart-beats. The same divine intelligence that makes the flower bloom. The same divine intelligence that makes the caterpillar turn into the butterfly. The moment we remember this fundamental truth is when oneness transforms from being a concept to being the only true reality that exists! So now I'm going to ask you a question -- Why are you here? Why do you exist in the form that you do right now, in this present moment?

Interestingly enough, all answers will eventually deduce one fundamental truth: TO UNITE. Simply look at nature, and then you will understand. The human body is made up of many different organs and cells. They all look different. They all have different functions. Yet they all work together to create a healthy body full of balance and harmony! Even though we know this, many of us judge each other by our differences instead of honoring each other's differences. Imagine if the heart said to the kidney, *"You look different from me so I'm not going to work with you anymore."* Imagine the brain saying that to the liver. Imagine the liver said that to the spleen. The body would experience DIS-EASE. Our world is in chaos because this is what we do to each other. We must embody true harmony and order if we want true harmony and order. If we can start by doing that within ourselves, that resonance will extend and radiate into the world around us! May we unite as one, and may we always remember that UNITY does not mean we all agree and are the same. UNITY simply means that we honor and respect each other's differences!

Dissolving Darkness

With this in mind, I'd like to express the vision that I see for humanity as we evolve into more spiritually elevated beings. Firstly, I'd like to share a foundational idea that my vision is built on. I have heard many people express that they believe that there is inherent evil within humanity and that this is *"Just the way it is."* My vision for our future is built on a different foundation of thought. I, for one, don't believe that evil is *"Just a part of human nature."* I know that it isn't, and I can very clearly explain why so you can understand this truth as well. We must first ask ourselves, what is evil? What is greed? What is corruption? What is hate? What is fear? These *'things'* are simply different vibrations and frequencies that we experience as a reality. The truth is that every reality is tuned to a different frequency and vibration. So just like evil, greed, corruption, hate, and war all operate at certain vibrations and frequencies, so do happiness, love, joy, gratitude, and Unity! Therefore, what makes us experience division over Unity, fear over love, selfishness vs. selflessness? The answer to this question is very simple. It all has to do with the vibrational frequency we, as a collective, are tuned to. So do evil and division always have to be a part of the human experience? Absolutely not.

Suppose we want to dissolve it from our experience. In that case, we must simply tune out of resonance with it and into resonance with a world that embodies Unity, collaboration, unconditional love, and selflessness. A world that I connected to through universal awareness. A world that is preoccupied with the spirit world as opposed to the physical world. A world that is connected to the Godly and Divine light that is inherent within everything that IS. So now the question is, *"How do we change the frequency we are tuned to?"* And once again, the answer is very simple. You see, it's one thing to express my vision for the future of humanity. It's another to show you how we can practically get there.

Tuning Your Vibration Of Being

Your vibration of being is made up of everything you do and, therefore, everything you are. Your words. Your thoughts. Your beliefs. Your friends. Your music. Your art. Your food. Your job. All of it! It all contributes to what eventually creates what we call your *'vibration of being.'* It is important because your vibration directly expresses what frequency you are tuned into and, therefore, what lens you will be experiencing your life through. The lens through which you experience life is what determines the reality that you experience! So, if everything makes up our vibration of being, where do we begin? To make this easy to understand, I will break this up into two portions: internal methods and external methods.

Internal Methods

Let's begin with internal methods of tuning up your vibration of being. When referring to *"Internal Methods,"* I refer to your words, thoughts, and beliefs. It's important to understand that, internally, your mind works according to *'programming,'* which is made up of your thoughts and your beliefs. Your *'external'* life is essentially a reflection of your mind's program and vice versa. Therefore, if you can shift your mind's program, you can shift your internal vibration of being, allowing you to experience a whole new reality externally. So how do we go about shifting our minds in programming? Once again, it is simple! We begin with our words. Why? Because words are the expression of your thoughts and your beliefs. Therefore, paying attention to the words that come out of your mouth is a very clever tool that you can use to read your mind's program, which comprises your thoughts and beliefs. It's also important to understand that words are vibrations, literally. The words you speak, over time, will imprint your mind program and form new thoughts and beliefs.

Therefore, it is very important to understand certain laws in your speech to succeed in using your internal methods of shifting your vibration of being.

Some laws of speech include:

1 The universe does not hear the word *'Not.'*
2 *'I want'* implies you don't already have
3 *'I will'* place something in the future which doesn't exist

So, where does this leave us? It leaves us with *"I AM."* So long as you use your speech consciously and presently, tuning into the reality you choose to experience it is easy! Simply acknowledge that you already have what you desire to experience, place it in your present moment, and focus on what you desire instead of what you don't!

External Methods

For some, the internal methods may be difficult. The good news is that there is a whole other aspect to this that you can rely on, known as the *'External Methods'* comprising everything in your day-to-day life, including your friends, music, art, books, etc. Everything! First and foremost, it is important to understand the connection between the internal and the external. The truth is, both of these are the same. The illusion is that they are separate because that is how we experience them in our day-to-day life.

Still, when we understand they are one and the same, we understand that internal change affects the external and vice versa. It means that if you are not good with changing the internal, focus on the external. If you're not good at changing the external, focus on the internal. For example, your mind is full of non-stop thoughts, and you don't know how to organize those thoughts through internal methods. Look around you and see what you can clean and organize in a place where you spend a lot of your time, perhaps your bedroom or your office.

Generally, if your mind is messy, the place you spend a lot of time in will also be messy. It's just the way it works. Remember, the internal and the external are a reflection of each other. If you don't know how to organize the mind, simply begin organizing and cleaning up your space, and the mind will slowly but surely become at ease once again. At this point, you may be thinking, *"It can't be that easy!"* But it is! It is that easy. As above, so below. As within, so without. It's all the same. Pay attention to everything in your external reality. The friends you attract. The music you listen to. The food that you eat. Ask yourself, *"Is this an expression of the 'Optimal' me?"* If it is, keep it in your surroundings. If it isn't, it's time to move on!

Manifesting The Vision

So why am I sharing this with you right now? I am sharing this with you because if I simply shared my vision for the future of humanity without giving pointers on how to get there, what's it worth? Additionally, I intend to show you how easy it is to manifest this incredible vision I have for the world that I'm sure we all share. We can most definitely live in a world of light, peace, and love. A world of harmony. A world where we all look out for each other. A world where no one has to lose for someone else to gain. A world that is truly connected to and through universal awareness. If we can constantly hold this vision while taking accountability for our own decisions and then taking appropriate action to manifest this vision, then it will come to fruition a whole lot sooner than you think!

Love, Jason

SAYING:

"I thought of a labyrinth of labyrinths, of one sinuous spreading labyrinth that would encompass the past and the future and in some way involve the stars."

— Jorge Luis Borges

JASON SHURKA

ABOUT THE AUTHOR

A Real Estate Investor & Entrepreneur turned Humanitarian.

At 24-year-old Jason Shurka decided to change his course to make a bigger difference in the world for the betterment of humanity.

Jason is passionate about bringing together (or UNIFYING) people worldwide and taking the steps together towards creating a world of Unity by putting the power back into the hands of the people. Aside from producing a 2-part documentary, three original series, and countless interviews seen by millions worldwide, Jason founded UNIFYD - a brand new censorship-free social media platform run BY the people, FOR the people. UNIFYD is unlike any other social media platform and is completely supported by users without the need for advertisers or investors.

Jasonshurka.com

17

UNFOLDING DREAMS, LOVE & PEACE

BY: RICKY PETERSON, AKA R'SI

"Love is All There Is"

Come and join the vision see,
What we will make humanity to be.
Dreams unfolding, peace and harmony,
Hear the beat of truth, its a love party.
Dancing, clap and sing, a world of love to bring.

Don't try to quench the flames of my heart,
I am a love warrior.
Don't try to change the sound of my march,
I am a love warrior.
To me love is the game and baba is the name.
It will inspire inner change.

Nows the time, don't delay,
Be a love soldier, we've got a world to change.

Come and see these, waterfalls,
Take a look at the showers in my eyes, they are
Tears of joy, no pain, becoming love insane

Baba Nam Kevalam, love is all there is
All around, can't hide, its here.
Remember, just, one simple phrase.
"Love is all there is."

RICKY PETERSON, AKA RS'I

ABOUT THE AUTHOR

A recent transplant to North Carolina, ***Rs'i*** earned his MBA in West Virginia, was born in California, and has both lived and traveled overseas. In addition to acting as CEO of his newly co-founded Information Technology (IT) consultancy firm, ***Shooting Stars Consulting***, he also works as the Registrar of the Neohumanist College of Asheville. He is passionate about spirituality and has been practicing Astaunga Yoga and a sentient-conscious diet for nearly two decades. He feels closest to his life purpose at this special moment in human history. He is grateful for the opportunity to be an instrument of that Supreme Cosmic Entity through sharing his lyrical composition.

18

BECOME AN AUTHOR
AT RADHAA PUBLISHING HOUSE

JOIN US!

BECOME an AUTHOR, or A CONTRIBUTING WRITER

R*adhaa Publishing House* is a holistic publishing company that focuses on helping heart-centered, mind-expanding, truth-telling authors get their work out into the world. Our focus is on collaborative book series and memoirs. We thrive on supporting our authors and contributing writers throughout this journey, empowering them to step into their divine and authentic voice while sharing their truth with the world. We especially celebrate cultural diversity worldwide, and we believe in weaving international voices to come together.

.
.
.

How are we different?

Many collaborative publishing companies bundle the authors together so that they don't receive individual credit and acknowledgment. We make sure each Author is seen and heard and can be found easily. This has led to authors telling us that they have received more traffic and business and clients on their websites. In a sense, each of the Book we create is also like a Directory highlighting contributing writers unique offerings. This has been a win-win for the contributing writers and authors.

Here is what our Authors have said about working with us:

"I felt totally supported. The best bit was feeling like being part of a loving family who wants you to be your best, do your best, and is there for you every step of the way. It also boosted my confidence as a writer. The collaborative nature of the project also made it way more fun than doing things alone". ***- Arrameia, Prague***

"Visibility was a big piece of me coming out of the spiritual closet, and I felt that Radhaa Publishing House has a high energy and integrity level. Both of which are important for light workers and Starseeds. The curators and authors are light workers. Radhaa Publishing House created this wonderful opportunity for many others to be a part of. I felt that they put their whole heart into making this happen even before, during, and after the book is published. It was a project that was totally supportive that made me feel safe to share myself and my story." ***- Lalitah, Turkey***

"It was wonderful to work with Radhaa Publishing House. I saw the effort and perseverance the whole team has and the support system they have for all the authors. I have matured as an author from this experience. I was so inspired after writing my chapter in this book, Awakening Starseeds, that I wrote an entire book called The Great Awakening because I was deeply moved writing."

- Leshara, Philippines

"My story was edited by Radhaa Publishing House, and let me tell you, it put me in tears! They made it better than the way I originally wrote and submitted it while keeping my story and voice true to its events. I read it, and tears just flowed because it was so good!"

- Cristal, Florida

"I have published many books on Consciousness, empowerment subjects, and relationships, but I had never revealed raw, real stories of my life as with Awakening Starseeds. I wanted to join other authors writing personal stories, and Radhaa Publishing House made it simple and empowering to share from my heart in a real, raw way. This team of conscious, awesome Starseeds encourages a revolution to Awaken other Starseeds worldwide!"

- Stasia, Utah

"This is an opportunity to STEP OUT, SPEAK OUR TRUTHS.

This is our time, an obligation to share and support others that live in fear and question their soul paths, their soul journey."

- Breda, Canada

At ***Radhaa Publishing House***, we are highly involved in the entire process and work personally with the authors to navigate authorship challenges.

Our authors are heart-centered, soul-driven, and ready to manifest their legacy. We acknowledge the courage and strength it takes to step out into the public eye, and our team is here to support you all the way.

Creating a book is a tedious process and requires persistence, patience, and perspective. There are many moving parts of the book that need attention, and our team knows how to work hard to ensure we can come through with flying colors for the final date of our release.

Step into your voice and be heard now! When you become a contributing writer or an author of Radhaa Publishing House, you empower yourself in a way you may have never experienced before. That's what our authors tell us. Claim your author power now!

"Be that change you wanted to be in our world!"

If you have a compelling story to share with the world, dream of being a published author, and wish to be a part of the Radhaa Publishing family, reach out to us.

"No other publishing company offers you in-house support the way that Radhaa Publishing House does. Your legacy awaits!"

You Make a Difference When You Support Our Holistic Books!

Published Books:

Awakening Starseeds: Shattering Illusions, Vol.1
Awakening Starseeds: Stories Beyond The Stargate, Vol. 2
Awakening Starseeds: Dreaming into the Future, Vol. 3
Pillars of Light: Stories of Goddess Activations™
Energy Healing & Soul Medicine
Quan Yin Goddess Activations™ Healing Workbook

Upcoming Books:

Infinite Cosmic Records: Doorways to Healing & Remembering
Memoirs of a Galactic Goddess Vol. 1
Memoirs of Galactic Goddess Vol. 2
Descendants of Lemuria

Where you can find Radhaa Publishing House Books:

Amazon.com — Barnes and Noble — Target
Walmart — Powell Books — Radhaa Publishing House &
Online Store: https://radhaanilia.net/shop/
OR Email: RadhaaPublishing@gmail.com

To find out more information about how to Join us, Become an Author or See our Upcoming Books, Please visit our Website at:

www.RadhaaPublishingHouse.com
Email: RadhaaPublishing@gmail.com

TO OUR READERS:

Dear Reader,

If you like our book, "**Awakening Starseeds: Dreaming Into The Future, Vol. 3,**" please support us by leaving a review on Amazon.

REVIEW us ONLINE at: Amazon.com
for "AWAKENING STARSEEDS: DREAMING INTO THE FUTURE, Vol. 3" book. We cannot do this without your support! Share this journey with us.

With Love & Gratitude, Thank you!

Join us 2023 for our 4th Volume of
Awakening Starseeds: Solutions For a Better Future

Thank you for your support! —*Radhaa*

CPSIA information can be obtained
at www.ICGtesting.com
Printed in the USA
JSHW052114201122
33572JS00002B/9

9 781952 124082